Larry VandeCreek, DMin
Arthur M. Lucas, MDiv
Editors

The Discipline
for Pastoral Care Giving:
Foundations for Outcome
Oriented Chaplaincy

The Discipline for Pastoral Care Giving: Foundations for Outcome Oriented Chaplaincy has been co-published simultaneously as *Journal of Health Care Chaplaincy*, Volume 10, Number 2 2001 and Volume 11, Number 1, 2001.

Pre-Publication
REVIEWS,
COMMENTARIES,
EVALUATIONS . . .

"**T**his volume edited by Larry VandeCreek and Arthur M. Lucas pulls together the extraordinary work of Arthur M. Lucas and his staff at Barnes-Jewish Hospital in St. Louis in the development of a new method of pastoral care called *The Discipline*. Lucas and his disciples describe a method of identifying patterns of coping in patients and spiritual interventions by chaplains that can be clearly communicated to other members of the health care team. This volume is likely to be an essential element in the continuing development of pastoral care methodologies in health care throughout the country."

Stanley J. Mullin, DMin
Director
Chaplaincy Service/Pastoral Education
Clarian Health Partners
Indianapolis, Indiana

"*The Discipline for Pastoral Care Giving* is about a concept called outcome based pastoral care. In my seminary education, which included CPE, we never learned about this topic, but in the new millennium chaplains will be expected to operate in outcome based systems. The last few years have brought significant changes to the field of health care, and many chaplains have struggled, to define, implement and integrate these new concepts into our practice of ministry. Most had to start without a model. In this book, we are given a model about one pastoral care department's response to the issue. Their model is a good place to start and it provides us with a framework with which to continue our dialogue about professional practice issues in chaplaincy."

Larry J. Austin, DMin
ACPE Supervisor, BCC
Director of Spiritual Care
Shore Health System of Maryland

"For the past ten years, Art Lucas and colleagues at Barnes-Jewish Hospital in St. Louis have been developing a cutting edge approach to spiritual care. It begins with a simple spiritual assessment, followed by specifying desired outcomes, intervention, and evaluation. In these papers, Lucas and colleagues describe the model and the issues they wrestled with in developing it, including the tension between being present and outcome focused care. Staff chaplains report how they incorporated the model in their speciality areas. Other papers describe using the model in clinical pastoral education. Implementing the model at Barnes-Jewish has led to greater recognition of the importance of chaplains in total patient care. This work is an essential resource for any chaplain who would like to be more intentional and explicit about the contribution of their care to patient outcomes."

George Fitchett, DMin
Associate Professor
and Director of Research
Rush-Presbyterian-St. Luke's
Medical Center
Chicago, Illinois

"The exciting approach to outcome oriented chaplaincy, articulately described in this volume, represents a novel and cogent strategy for strengthening the contributions that chaplains can make to patient care. The authors describe *The Discipline*, a stepwise approach to developing a spiritual profile of a patient, identifying shared outcomes, constructing a logical plan for reaching those outcomes, and assessing whether these outcomes have been achieved. By focusing their model on specific disease states rather than denominational-affiliations, the authors make a compelling case for the commonality in how spirit functions in a given clinical context. After describing *The Discipline*, the authors present thoughtful descriptions of its application in various clinical and educational contexts. Particularly admirable is *The Discipline's* commitment to developing concrete outcomes for pastoral care and its honest and straightforward strategy for determining whether these outcomes have been achieved. A must read for those interested in ensuring that pastoral care remains an integral part of health care delivery in the 21st century."

Thomas H. Gallagher, MD
Assistant Professor of Medicine
Washington University School
of Medicine
St. Louis, Missouri

"Those who are interested in the care of the whole person in health care settings often live in the tension between unfolding process and measurable outcomes, stories and numbers, being and doing, faith and proof. *The Discipline for Pastoral Care Giving: Foundations for Outcome Oriented Chaplaincy* addresses those tensions directly and offers a model for health professionals wanting to transcend those classic dualities. While remaining faithful to personal narratives and meanings, this work does not back away from discussions of method and measurement. *The Discipline* offers readers knowledge and tools for a rigorous professional intentionality, for a more precise communication of a discipline's activities to the health care team, and most importantly, for responsive and responsible care giving. Upon reading this volume, one is left with the realization that it is in relationship, in lived moments of care giving, that one knows best how people can claim and work together toward outcomes of healing."

Valerie J. Yancey, RN, PhD
Associate Professor
Jewish Hospital College
of Nursing and Allied Health
St. Louis, Missouri

"In today's turbulent health care market, health administrators and care givers are struggling to balance missions and margins.

Having worked alongside many of the gifted pastoral care professional's in this volume, I can attest to the important role they play in ensuring American health care keeps focused on our primary mission to care for our patients and communities. Pastoral care is no longer a service of our health care system, it's an integral part of it. When we created BJC Health System in St. Louis, our pastoral care teams were front and center in helping us create an atmosphere of trust and compassion. Spiritual care continues to gain the recognition and respect it deserves.

The Discipline for Pastoral Care Giving is a must for any health care administrator's bookshelf."

Fred L. Brown, FACHE
Vice Chairman
BJC Health System
St. Louis, Missouri
Visiting Professor
George Washington University

The Discipline
for Pastoral Care Giving:
Foundations
for Outcome Oriented
Chaplaincy

The Discipline for Pastoral Care Giving: Foundations for Outcome Oriented Chaplaincy has been co-published simultaneously as *Journal of Health Care Chaplaincy,* Volume 10, Number 2 2001 and Volume 11, Number 1 2001.

The Discipline
for Pastoral Care Giving:
Foundations
for Outcome Oriented
Chaplaincy

Larry VandeCreek, DMin
Arthur M. Lucas, MDiv
Editors

The Discipline for Pastoral Care Giving: Foundations for Outcome Oriented Chaplaincy has been co-published simultaneously as *Journal of Health Care Chaplaincy,* Volume 10, Number 2 2001 and Volume 11, Number 1 2001.

Routledge
Taylor & Francis Group
New York London

The Discipline for Pastoral Care Giving: Foundations for Outcome Oriented Chaplaincy has been co-published simultaneously as *Journal of Health Care Chaplaincy*™, Volume 10, Number 2 2001 and Volume 11, Number 1 2001.

The development, preparation, and publication of this work has been undertaken with great care. However, the publisher, employees, editors, and agents of The Haworth Press and all imprints of The Haworth Press, Inc., including The Haworth Medical Press® and Pharmaceutical Products Press®, are not responsible for any errors contained herein or for consequences that may ensue from use of materials or information contained in this work. Opinions expressed by the author(s) are not necessarily those of The Haworth Press, Inc.

Cover figure reprinted with permission ©Arthur M. Lucas.

Cover design by Thomas J. Mayshock Jr.

Library of Congress Cataloging-in-Publication Data

The discipline for pastoral care giving : foundations for outcome oriented chaplaincy / Larry Vande-Creek, Arthur M. Lucas, editors.
     p. cm.
     "Has been co-published simultaneously as Journal of health care chaplaincy, volume 10, number 2, 2001, and volume 11, number 1, 2001."
     Includes bibliographical references and index.
     ISBN 0-7890-1345-2 (alk. paper) – ISBN 0-7890-1346-0 (alk. paper)
     1. Pastoral theology. I. VandeCreek, Larry. II. Lucas, Arthur M.
[DNLM: 1. Pastoral Care.]
BV4011 .D53 2001
259'.4–dc21

2001024047

The Discipline for Pastoral Care Giving: Foundations for Outcome Oriented Chaplaincy

CONTENTS

CURRENT CONTENTS IN THE LITERATURE
OF INTEREST TO PASTORAL CARE

ABOUT THE EDITORS

Larry VandeCreek, DMin, BCC, is Director of Pastoral Research at The HealthCare Chaplaincy in New York City. For 23 years, he held faculty and staff positions with The Ohio State University College of Medicine and Public Health and its associated medical center. Dr. VandeCreek is a member of numerous professional associations including the Association of Professional Chaplains, Inc., the American Association of Pastoral Counselors, and the Association for Clinical Pastoral Education. He has published many journal articles which examine aspects of the relationship between religious faith and illness. Dr. VandeCreek is the author of *A Research Primer for Pastoral Care and Counseling* (Journal of Pastoral Care Publications, 1988) and is Co-Editor of *The Chaplain-Physician Relationship* (1991). He is Editor of the *Journal of Health Care Chaplaincy* (The Haworth Press, Inc.) which has published *Ministry of Hospital Chaplains: Patient Satisfaction* (1997), *Scientific and Pastoral Perspectives on Intercessory Prayer: An Exchange Between Larry Dossey, M.D. and Health Care Chaplains* (1998), *Spiritual Care for Persons with Dementia: Fundamentals for Pastoral Practice* (1999), *Contract Pastoral Care and Education: The Trend of the Future?* (1999), and *Professional Chaplaincy: What Is Happening to It During Health Care Reform?* (2000).

Arthur M. Lucas, MDiv, BCC, is Director of Spiritual Care Services for Barnes-Jewish Hospital at Washington University Medical Center, St. Louis, Missouri. He is a United Methodist ordained Elder and Endorsed Chaplain, an Association of Professional Chaplains Board Certified Chaplain (BCC) and an Association for Clinical Pastoral Education (ACPE) Certified Supervisor. In 1976 he founded the Pastoral Care Department at Methodist Medical Center in St. Joseph, Missouri, building an Association for Clinical Pastoral Education accredited CPE program and eventually a pastoral counseling service. When Methodist Medical Center merged with the other St. Joseph hospital to form Heartland Health System, Chaplain Lucas was named the Executive Director of the new department. In time, he became leader of a new division that included inpatient and outpatient mental health services, chemical dependence services, employee assistance programming as well as pastoral care and pastoral counseling. Since coming to Barnes-Jewish in 1990 he has led the development of the hospital's Spiritual Care Department into a person centered, discipline based, outcome oriented professional service.

CURRENT CONTENTS IN THE LITERATURE OF INTEREST TO PASTORAL CARE

Introduction

W. Noel Brown, STM, BCC, Editor

In 1972, a book was published that more than any other has become a catalyst for change in the field of health care. This book, *Effectiveness and Efficiency: Random Reflections on Health Services* by Archie L. Cochrane, threw a spotlight on the collective ignorance of the medical profession concerning the effects of their practices. The book was to spark a revolution that in the quarter century since its appearance has begun to provide physicians with accurate information about the results of their medical and surgical practices, encouraging them to practice information-based medicine. The Cochrane Collaboration, as it is now called, has become a worldwide, voluntary collaboration by health care professionals who offer their skill and time, working in one of more than forty groups that review what physicians around the world are reporting that they do when they practice medicine.

W. Noel Brown is ACPE Chaplain Supervisor, Department of Case Management, Northwestern Memorial Hospital, 250 East Huron Street, Chicago, IL 60611 (E-mail: nbrown@nmh.org). He is also Editor and Publisher of *The Orere Source.*

In preparing the bibliography below, my thoughts kept returning to the Cochrane Collaboration. I believe that health care chaplains are approaching the time when we will have to begin our own "Cochrane Collaboration." It will be a time in which we will have to examine what exactly we do as chaplains, what exactly happens when we do it, and whether or not it is of value.

I am under no illusions as to the difficulty of this task. I can hear some concerns being voiced already. "Clergy are not comfortable having their work scrutinized." "What we do in ministry is a sacred task–it should not be subject to investigative probing, especially by secular examiners." "But would it be ethical? Surely people of the faith community will not welcome scientific scrutiny!" And then there is the voice of the trained and qualified chaplain; "I am a Board Certified Chaplain. I know what I am doing." The objections have a familiar sound to any who have read this literature because they parallel those of many in the medical profession a quarter century ago. Our professional training has not prepared us well for this task. Our employers may be reluctant to allow us some time to do the required work, but the data gathering and scrutiny must be done. Despite our best efforts in training, supervision, and accreditation we will find, as did the medical profession, that our practices are often driven by custom, hearsay, and dogma.

The existing medical and chaplaincy literature contains material that will be of help to us. The bibliographic material that follows can inform and assist us. The references are divided into five sections grouped somewhat thematically. We begin with a collection of articles describing the Cochrane Collaboration itself, how it began, some of the important objections that were raised concerning the project, and what it has been able to accomplish.

Second, I cite a collection of articles from the pastoral care literature. In these papers, some chaplains as well as supporters of the profession urge that we become more outcome oriented in our thinking and practice. This literature began at a time when hospitals first felt the squeeze of economic reform. There were a number of far-sighted persons who quickly saw that chaplaincy might be endangered by such reforms. They urged chaplains to identify what they were doing and to be prepared to show the economic value their ministry represented within health care settings. While this argument about economic value holds even today, it has been joined by a second reason–all health care team members now focus their thinking and activity in this way.

Third is a collection of articles that report what chaplains actually do in their ministry, or, outcome-oriented results of pastoral care. While the results are preliminary in nature they are useful because they show that outcome-oriented thinking can be done by chaplains. The findings about what chaplains actually do in their ministry are foundational for future research.

The fourth category contains studies of very great importance although currently few in number. They describe intervention methods that reflect selected chaplaincy responses to health care reform. This section, hopefully, will expand in the future to include the materials that follow in this volume.

The final section contains a number of papers intended to help chaplains think about research methodologies that are compatible with the "people-oriented" ways in which we minister. They are methodologies that are based in values of justice and democracy and sit comfortably within a broad Judeo-Christian theological framework.

Within CPE training and the chaplaincy accreditation processes of the 21st century, the major question asked of students has always been "Who are you?" (See the first objective of Introductory CPE in the current Standards of the ACPE.) Based on the belief that self-knowledge was central for effective pastoral ministry, preparation for chaplaincy has suffered from the lack of an other-directedness. Outcomes were not on the agenda of CPE students during the 20th century. It is a time for a more balanced approach. Self-understanding must be joined by a focus on outcomes.

CURRENT CONTENTS IN THE LITERATURE OF INTEREST TO PASTORAL CARE

The Cochrane Collaboration

Archie L. Cochrane.
The history of the measurement of ill health International.
J of Epidemiology, 1(# 2) (Summer 1972), 89-92.

Georginia Ferry.
Between what we know and what we do: the Cochrane collaboration.
HMSBeagle, 14 (5 Sept 1997), 1-5.

Sharon Kingman.
Quality control for medicine.
New Scientist, 143 (# 1943) (17 Sept 1994) 22-26.

Stanley J. Reiser.
The era of the patient: using the experience of illness in shaping the missions of health care.
JAMA, 269(# 8) (24 Feb 1993), 1012-1017.

Gary Taubes.
Looking for the evidence in medicine.
Science, 272 (5 Apr 1996), 22-24.

Harry P. Wetzler.
A way to measure value.
Healthcare Forum Journal, 37(# 4) (Jul/Aug 1994), 45-49.

Chaplains (and Others) Urging the Development of Outcomes-Based Chaplaincy

Gary E. Berg.
A statement on clinical assessment for pastoral care.
Chaplaincy Today, 14(# 2) (1998), 42-50.

Graeme D. Gibbons.
Pastoral care case mix codings: an attempt to integrate theology, the clinical pastoral education and hospital ministry traditions with recent developments in information technology.
Ministry Society and Theology, 10(# 1) (July 1996), 44-65.

Graeme D. Gibbons.
Developing codes for pastoral diagnoses and pastoral responses in hospital chaplaincy.
Chaplaincy Today, 14(# 1) (1998), 4-13.

Fred Gifford.
Outcome research and practice guidelines: upstream issues for downstream users.
Hastings Center Report, 26(# 2) (Mar/Apr 1996), 38-44.

Terese Hudson.
Measuring the results of faith.
Hospitals and Health Networks, 70(# 18) (20 Sept 1996), 23-28.

Bonnie M. Jennings & Nancy Staggers.
The language of outcomes.
Advances in Nursing Science, 20(# 4) (June 1998), 72-80.

W. Brad Johnson.
Outcome research and religious psychotherapies: where are we and where are we going?
Journal of Psychology and Theology, 21(# 4) (Winter 1993), 297-308.

Timothy E. Madison.
Can chaplaincy be sold without selling out?
Chaplaincy Today, 14(# 2), (1998), 3-8.

Elisabeth McSherry & William A. Nelson.
The DRG era: a major opportunity for increasing pastoral input: or crisis?
Journal of Pastoral Care, 41(# 3) (Sept 1987), 201-212.

Elisabeth McSherry.
The crisis in health care: pastoral care in the DRG world.
ACPE Conference Proceedings (Oct 1986), 28-50.

Elisabeth McSherry.
Outpatient care: the modern chaplains' new impact in healthcare reform.
Journal of Health Care Chaplaincy, 6(# 1) (1994), 83-108.

Elisabeth McSherry.
Pastoral care: more necessary in the DRG era.
Health Care Management Review, 11(# 1) (1986), 47-59.

Articles Reporting Outcome-Oriented Results of Care

John L. Florell.
Crisis intervention in orthopedic surgery–empirical evidence of the effectiveness of a chaplain working with surgery patients.
Bulletin of the A.P.H.A. 37(# 2) (1973), 29-36.

Graeme D. Gibbons, Andrew Retsas, & Jaya Pinikahana.
Describing what chaplains do in hospitals.
Journal of Pastoral Care, 53(# 2) (Summer 1999), 201-207.

Will Kinnaird & Elisabeth McSherry.
The development and use of codes for chaplain interventions,
(procedures and products) in the Veterans Affairs
Healthcare System.
Chaplaincy Today, 14(# 1) (1998), 14-22.

Thomas St. J. O'Connor, Karen-Anne Fox, Elizabeth Meakes & Glenn
Empey.
Quantitative and qualitative outcome research on a regional basic
supervised SPE program.
Journal of Pastoral Care, 51(# 2) (Summer 1997), 195-206.

Steven R. Salisbury, M.R. Ciulla, & Elisabeth McSherry.
Clinical management reporting and objective diagnostic instruments
for spiritual assessment in spinal chord injury patients.
Journal of Health Care Chaplaincy, 2(# 3) (1989), 35-55.

Renee Twombly.
Use of prayer or Noetic therapy may contribute to better outcomes.
In the News, Duke University Medical Center (9 Nov 1998), 1-2.

Larry VandeCreek & Marjorie Lyons.
Ministry of hospital chaplains: patient satisfaction.
J of Health Care Chaplaincy (US), 6(# 2) (1997), 1-61.

Larry VandeCreek & Marjorie Lyons.
The general hospital chaplain's ministry; analysis of productivity,
quality and cost.
Care Giver Journal, 11(# 2) (1994-5), 3-11.

Larry VandeCreek & Art M. Lucas.
Defining the value of pastoral care services: research strategies related
to the patient's coping process.
Care Giver Journal, 11(# 1-2) (1994), 13-26.

Robert J. Yim & Larry VandeCreek.
Unbinding grief and life's losses for thriving recovery after open heart
surgery: how pastoral care works in the managed care setting.
Care Giver Journal, 12(# 2) (1996), 8-11.

Intervention Methods Being Used

Steven R. Hawks, Melisa L. Hull, Rebecca L. Thalman, & Paul M. Richins.
Review of spiritual health: definition, role and intervention strategies.
Am. J. of Health Promotion, 9(# 5) (May/Jun 1995), 371-378.

Swindell Hodges.
Spiritual screening: the starting place for intentional pastoral care.
Chaplaincy Today, 15(# 1) (1999), 31-39.

Arthur M. Lucas, Julie A. Berger, Janet Crane, Lawrence Olatunde, & Robert Yim.
Fundamentals of outcomes-oriented spiritual care.
Unpublished monograph APC/NACC Conference (26 Feb 2000), 1-50.

Janice L. Wakefield, R. David Cox, & Janet S. Forrest.
Linking components of the pastoral continuum of care: admission screens, spiritual assessment, and chart documentation.
Proceedings, Joint APC/NACC Conference, (Feb 2000), 227-234.

Janice L. Wakefield, R. David Cox, & Janet S. Forrest.
Seeds of change: the development of a spiritual assessment model.
Chaplaincy Today, 15(# 1) (1999), 41-50.

Papers About Research That Have Implications for Pastoral Care

Paul Derrickson.
Computer coding of pastoral ministry: contributions and challenges.
Chaplaincy Today, 14(# 1) (1998), 23-26.

Robert J Gatchel & Ann M. Maddrey.
Clinical outcome research in complementary and alternative medicine: an overview of experimental design and analysis.
Alternative Therapies, 4(# 5) (Sept 1998), 36-42.

D. Richard Pohl & J.V. Porter.
Coping with the quality-cost-crunch.
Bulletin of the A.P.H.A., 34(# 2) (1975), 49-59.

J. & L. Lofland.
Analyzing the Social Setting: a guide to social observation and analysis.
Belmont, CA: Wadsworth (3rd ed. 1985).

Ann C. Macaulay, Laura E. Commanda, William L. Freeman, & Nancy Gibson.
Participatory research maximizes community and lay involvement.
British Medical Journal, 319(# 7212) (18 Sept 1999), 774-778.

Julienne Meyer.
Using qualitative methods in health related action research.
British Medical Journal, 320(# 7228) (15 Jan 2000), 178-181.

Catherine Pope, Sue Ziebland, & Nicholas Mays.
Analyzing qualitative data,
British Medical Journal, 320(# 7227) (8 Jan 2000), 114-116.

THE DISCIPLINE
FOR PASTORAL CARE GIVING

Introduction to *The Discipline* for Pastoral Care Giving

Arthur M. Lucas, MDiv, BCC

SUMMARY. During the last eight years, the professional chaplains of Spiritual Care Services at Barnes-Jewish Hospital-Washington University Medical Center (BJC) have developed a discipline based, outcome-oriented model for chaplaincy. This article introduces the elements of *The Discipline*, our development process, the effects on our chaplaincy attributable to its consistent use, and implications for the future. While many of our assumptions about chaplaincy have been challenged, our experience is that a disciplined, outcome-oriented model for chaplaincy has deepened our relationships with patients and significantly increased our integration into the care teams of the hospital. It has also challenged and enhanced our abilities to be emotionally present with patients while also giving attention to the process of the visits and chaplain interventions that contribute to patient healing and well-being.

The Reverand Arthur M. Lucas is Director, The Department of Spiritual Care Services, Barnes-Jewish Hospital at Washington University Medical Center, Mailstop #90-53-391, One Barnes-Jewish Plaza, St. Louis, MO 63110 (E-mail: AML2792@bjc.org).

1

KEYWORDS. Chaplain, pastoral care, measurement, outcomes, discipline

INTRODUCING BARNES-JEWISH SPIRITUAL CARE AS THE CONTEXT FOR THE DISCIPLINE

Since 1990, the chaplains at Barnes-Jewish Hospital (BJH) have sought to increase their integration into and accountability with the care teams. Carrying through these intentions led to far more than we anticipated.

We consciously maintained pastoral presence, relationship, and process at the core of our care. And we are now clear that our primary purpose is not simply to be in relationship to patients or aware of the process. Our purpose is to contribute to their healing and well-being, whatever that may mean for each of them. In the process of clarifying this for ourselves, we developed *The Discipline* and it greatly enhanced our integration and accountability in the clinical services for patients. And, more immediately, *The Discipline* enhanced our ability to engage the spirituality of the people in our care for their healing and well-being. We have also become more outcome-oriented, consciously attending to the effect of our care for our patients and families.

We entered this process with some value assertions and discovered others along the way. One assumption was that spiritual assessment was not about the size or good/bad of Spirit. Rather, we wanted to know how the spiritual functioned, what differences it made for and with the people in our care. We wanted to capture the difference it made in people's lives. Another assertion we made at the beginning was that, in this spiritual assessment process, each of us was more a partner with the person and their spirituality than someone who needed to make it "right." We were to perceive, respect, and engage this spirituality.

We immediately found that, when we emphasized these assertions in our pastoral care as well as our integration and accountability within the care teams, we also had to be more conscious of our pastoral care assessment, planning and reflection processes. We found that doing so led to:

1. *Evaluating and improving our care.* When we were more conscious of our pastoral presence and process, knew how we knew who was before us, and what effect we were having, then we were more able to change the care we were giving. Deliberate

evaluation either in the midst of the caring or upon reflection afterwards improved that care.

2. *Communicating our care more effectively with others.* With the process more conscious, we made choices in the language through which we organized and communicated both the spirituality of the people in our care and our chaplaincy with them. We were then able to help other members of the care team to provide more whole, personally efficacious care as well.

3. *Seeing patterns in the struggling, coping, and healing of people.* Health challenges, crisis, and treatment interventions seemed to be associated with discrete patterns. In a cumulative manner, we began to learn from patients/families about the unique spiritual dynamics associated with health care challenges as well as the spiritual care that seemed to hold the most promise for contributing to their healing and well-being.

From the beginning, several staff chaplains were involved in our development of *The Discipline.* They included Eric Affholter in HIV/AIDS Care, Robert Yim in Heart Services, Cheryl Palmer in Thoracic Services, and Julie Allen Berger in Oncology. Others joined us later, including Lawrence Olatunde in Trauma, Fred Smoot in Psychiatry, and Janet Crane in HIV/AIDS care. Each of us became more conscious of what we were learning from our clinical experience, more aware of what patients were teaching us cumulatively. Patterns emerged in the spiritual dynamics during life changing health care challenges as we looked at an individual case alongside the next, alongside the next, alongside the next, to the hundreds of clinically/diagnostically similar cases.

Our cumulative learning was enhanced (or perhaps made possible) by assigning individual chaplains to discrete clinical areas. This allowed each chaplain to focus on the spirituality of patients in distinct clinical contexts and identify patterns of spiritual challenges. These clinically similar patients provided us focused, repetitive opportunities to learn how best to engage their spirituality for optimum outcomes.

Cultivating a deliberate, disciplined reflection process also helped us see patterns. Rather than seeing only the uniqueness of each patient story, we began to see commonalities. We found similar spiritual dynamics for patients who were clinically similar even when they might be religiously dissimilar.

We began to observe three primary spirituality patterns among patients. The first concerned *how spirituality was operating.* The second focused on *the function of spirituality or what it was called on to do,* and third, *what effect spirituality seemed to have.* These three helped us see the similarities of the dynamic and the functional levels involved. Based on these patterns, we were able to focus more clearly and quickly on the critical spiritual dynamics for patients who were dealing with specific clinical realities in specific contexts. Focusing with intentionality made it easier for us to meet, honor and engage spirituality for patient healing and well-being.

Seeing these patterns reminded us of creative tensions in which we were now more consciously living. This first tension was between the unique individual on the one hand and generalizable dynamics on the other. Our previous training had taught us to distrust the general/universal and always depend on the particular, the unique, the individual for pastoral understanding. When we also began to see the spiritual commonalities, we felt bound to accept what individual patients taught us for the benefit of others. We still could not settle comfortably into "knowing" how all heart or cancer or thoracic patients "were." We still saw too much individuality, were surprised too many times, and still believed deeply in the richness of creation. Nor could we revert to self-induced ignorance about the experiences of patients so that we could overlook what they taught us. We were left with the creative tension between individuality and common patterns.

A second creative tension was between presence/process and doing/ outcomes. We had learned in seminary and/or CPE that doing "nothing" was a primary value of a pastoral care giver in health care. Phlebotomists, respiratory therapists, nurses, and doctors went into patient rooms with tools and technologies to do things. As pastors, we entered with our personal, emotional availability and tried to be "present" with patients. In that way, we assured our attentiveness to patient feelings, faith, personhood, and agenda as we tried to be faithful vessels of the Spirit, journeying with them. As taught, we embraced this lack of control and believed it provided a healing counterpoint to technologists. Unfortunately, the implication of not being in control, especially on the spiritual level, involved disowning intentionality. We avoided intentionality about what was likely to be good for patients because it would be controlling. Intentionality meant we were imposing values and agenda, putting predetermined criteria above the person just as we believed the science/technology-based caregivers were doing.

In our explorations, we found being present with patients can include informed intentionality. We found that the spiritual process of the pastoral visit can be enriched by attention to what we can contribute. If we intended good to come from our care, what good? As soon as we could identify the intended good, we were dealing with outcomes. More precisely, we were dealing with "contributing outcomes" because our contributions were among those made by all the other care givers.

Another way to understand "contributing outcome" is to think of the benefits contributed by every member of the health care team. Each contributes in their own way to a desired outcome that hopefully furthers patient well-being. The final outcome, of course, takes a variety of forms. It may mean a peaceful death, a meaningful life that integrates a chronic illness, or a return to a lifestyle that preceded the illness. For instance:

1. A well-done coronary artery bypass graft surgery has the promise of the "contributing outcome" of returning blood flow to the heart. The surgery is an activity (or intervention); the hoped for good (contributing outcome) is the return of blood flow to the heart which should contribute to an intended thriving recovery from heart disease.
2. A well-done radiation treatment series promises the "contributing outcome" of reducing the tumor size for a cancer patient. The radiation treatments are activities (or interventions), the hoped for good (contributing outcome) is the reduction of the tumor which should contribute to an intended remission or reduction of the cancer in the patient's life.

As we built *The Discipline,* we experienced the profound challenge of giving attention at the same time to both contributing outcomes and the more traditional process orientation. We were stretched both conceptually and personally by our attempts to hold these two in tension.

Notice that the idea of control was excluded from our resolution of this core tension. We concluded that it is a seductive fantasy in any framework. The challenge is to look elsewhere for substance and accountability.

Resolving either of these two tensions described above by going to one of the poles now seemed insufficient. The reality of the patient's life changing situation outstripped the coziness of either pole. The complexity of what it took to be a caring presence in those realities denied the simple comforts of certainty offered by either pole. We learned we could live and thrive without the polar comforts once we realized that none of this was really about us, the care givers. It was about those in our care and their healing. That made the challenges and uncertainties of living within these tensions worthwhile and more appropriate to the real life complexities confronting our patients.

INTRODUCING THE DISCIPLINE FOR PASTORAL CARE GIVING

As the staff chaplains began to observe patterns among the patients, I, as department director, began to observe the patterns within the chaplaincy. The two processes began to feed each other. Even given the uniquenesses of staff chaplains and clinical contexts, a pattern ran through their most compassionate, faithful and effective care. The pattern in their chaplaincy became the basis for *The Discipline for Pastoral Care Giving.*

I will introduce each element of *The Discipline* separately and in more depth, but first, step back to see a sketch of the whole process as displayed in Figure 1.

- *The Discipline* always, always starts with the **Needs, Hopes, and Resources** of those to whom we are providing care, whether they are patients, residents, family, staff, ourselves, our students, or entire nursing units and departments. While the focus of our care always varies, our engagement always starts with attending to their Spiritual Needs/Hopes/Resources.
- Attending to Needs, Hopes and Resources provides the living material for developing a structurally consistent, **Profile** of the people to whom we providing care. By wondering how their faith functions in life and what differences their spirituality can make in their life changing situations, we sketch out their sense of the *Holy, Meaning, Hope and Community.*
- Once we are into the processes of getting to know people and organizing what we are learning, we focus on getting some idea of the **Desired Contributing Outcome(s)** for this patient/family. What can our ministry contribute to this person's healing and well-being? What difference do we hope to make?

- Once we have identified contributions we hope to make to the patient's healing, we develop and share a **Plan** for how we together can move toward those contributing outcomes and what our distinct pastoral role is in the plan.
- With a plan in mind we can provide specific **Interventions** based on that plan, specifically those unique to spiritual care.
- Then it is appropriate to **Measure** the actual outcomes of our care against the desired contributing outcomes we had in mind.
- And then, perhaps we need to cycle right back around to a new assessment of needs, hopes, and resources.

As you read more about each aspect of *The Discipline,* note that however specific or focused the components, it remains largely content free. It is a model awaiting each application. While it forms a map, a structure outlining the flow of the care giving, it is dependent on the patient/family for substance and applicability. We are partially alerted to that substance by what previous patients have graciously taught us. For the care of a person facing a health care crisis, the structure of *The*

FIGURE 1

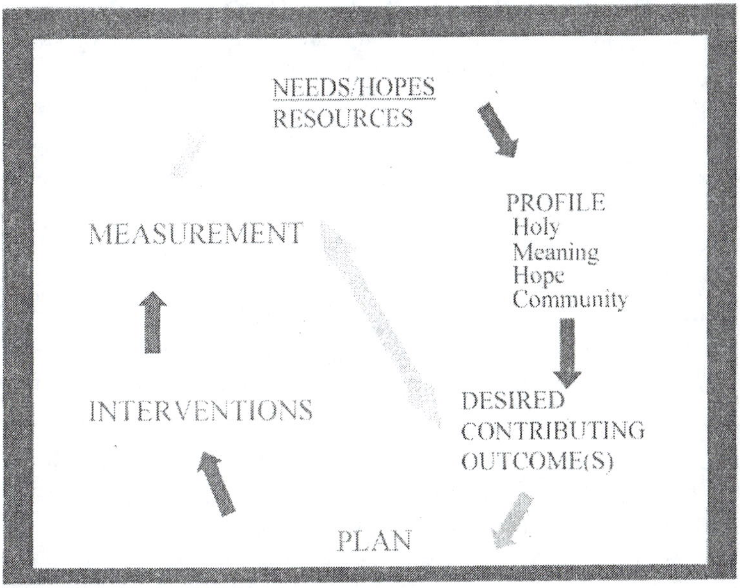

NEEDS/HOPES
RESOURCES

PROFILE
Holy
Meaning
Hope
Community

MEASUREMENT

DESIRED
CONTRIBUTING
OUTCOME(S)

INTERVENTIONS

PLAN

Discipline and the most carefully identified patterns are utterly dependent on the individual before us for substance and meaning. *The Discipline* only helps provide focus, communication, reflection, and accountability. Doing so then aids effectiveness.

Needs, Hopes, and Resources

The Discipline always starts with the Needs, Hopes and Resources of whomever is the focus of your care. The traditional approach starts with patient needs. The caregiver finds out the patient's needs based on their diagnosis and various assessments, and then, as a caring professional, takes care of those needs. That traditional approach casts the patient as a big bag of needs, and each caregiver, including the chaplain, as big bags of resources involved in a one-way repair and reclamation process. Starting with Needs, Hopes *and* Resources acknowledges that the patient has needs. It also acknowledges that they have *hopes* that provide energy, direction, impetus, and motivation for the future. Hopes draw the individual forward. The illness is part of that life. This means that the question becomes, "How can the chaplain help this patient cope with, integrate, or overcome this illness in a way that taps the extant energy present in the hopefulness?" Additionally, starting with Needs/Hopes/ Resources acknowledges that patients have *resources* available. Patients typically possess a wide variety of spiritual resources that were helpful to them up to the present moment. Ignoring those resources demeans the person, makes ministry more difficult (and our lives poorer), and lessens the availability of healing for patients and families. There are probably an endless variety of ways people make their spirituality available to us (Figure 2). The themes and key words in the stories patients tell contained in the figure allow us to hear their real spirituality. Vignettes within the stories are like open windows through which we can see their spirituality. The variety is large and caregivers must allow the patients to select the terms, themes, or windows through which they communicate. The chaplain must possess the skill to perceive the spirituality through the formats s/he makes available and begin to grasp, sort, organize and find the order within for our spiritual understanding of the Needs, Hopes and Resources.

FIGURE 2

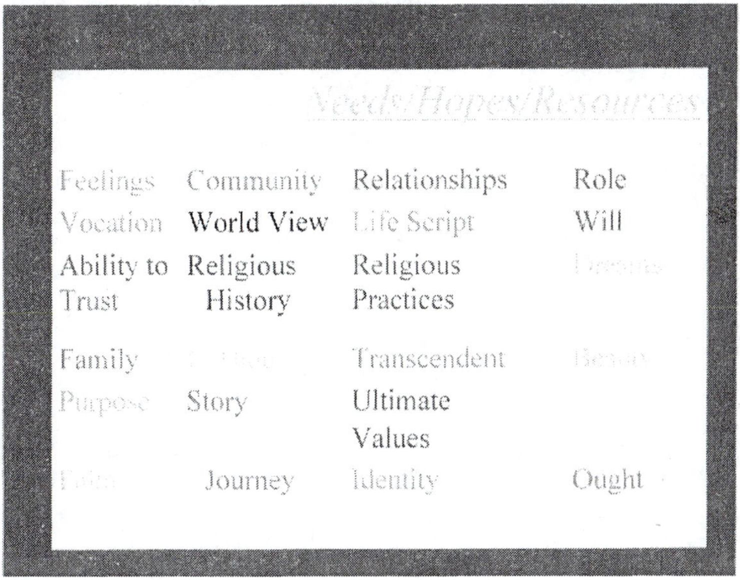

		Needs/Hopes/Resources	
Feelings	Community	Relationships	Role
Vocation	World View	Life Script	Will
Ability to Trust	Religious History	Religious Practices	
Family		Transcendent	
Purpose	Story	Ultimate Values	
	Journey	Identity	Ought

Profile

Patients share a wealth of material about themselves and the chaplain must organize it in ways that are useful and faithful to each individual in his/her care. Organizing this material in a consistent way facilitates communication among caregivers, raising the effectiveness of the entire care process. Chaplains need to be able to take the raw material and focus it around a set of touchstones, forming a Spiritual Profile.

We use the word "profile" very carefully. A profile is a two-dimensional representation of a three dimensional object. It is inadequate as a picture of the whole, but it is a piece of it. It is flat, without depth, but is at the same time worthwhile and often elegant. We emphasize that the persons to whom we are providing care are three-dimensional and dynamic. We are humbled when we recognize that we do not have the whole picture, but then, neither does anyone else on the health care team. All those disciplines develop their particular profiles, in their own ways, around their own foci. Without their profiles, our understanding of the person is inadequate. Without ours, their's is inadequate. For the doctor, nurse, physical therapist, dietitian, social worker or anyone else, a faithful and understandable spiritual profile is necessary in order to have a fuller picture of the person before them. For us to approach a full understanding of the person we need to incorporate all the other profiles available in the setting and the other professionals need to incorporate ours.

We organize all of the raw material about the person's spiritual Needs/Hopes/Resources around four particular points as displayed in Figure 3: the Sense of Holy, Meaning, Hope, and Community. In settling on those four we used a combination of:

- What we observed in our discussions about patients,
- What we read and learned from other chaplains who worked with spiritual assessment,[1,2] and
- What worked when we communicated with those in other disciplines?

The other disciplines helped us because, early in our efforts, we asked them what they counted on from us. We heard things about

FIGURE 3

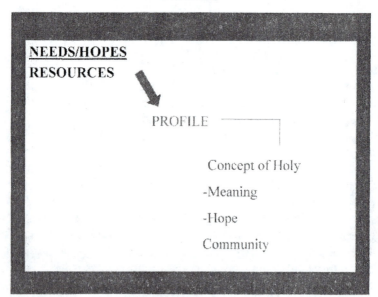

NEEDS/HOPES
RESOURCES

PROFILE

Concept of Holy

-Meaning

-Hope

Community

meaningfulness, hope, communities, families, and, of course, we heard about God.

But having a common language for a Profile was not sufficient because we needed a common understanding of what the language meant, what to listen for as we met patients, heard their stories, felt their impact on us, and began to assess their spiritual Needs/Hopes/ Resources. We established that commonality by giving attention to *function*: how do these components of the spiritual profile function, especially in this context. What difference do they make, and how?

Sense of the Holy

Here we begin with certain implicit questions concerning how a patient identifies herself religiously. The "how" and "what" questions are the most important for our dynamic assessment and care planning (Figure 4). How does she understand the Holy? How does she go about that understanding? What is the substance of that understanding in terms of her living life? How does the Holy function in her world? When she is more aware of the Holy in her world, how does the Holy make a difference and what is that difference? And when the Holy does function in her life, in her awareness, what tends to flow from that function? When she is more aware of the Holy in her life, does she feel resourced? Is she reminded of her goodness, createdness, and the resources of being human? Is she humble if she is more aware of the Holy? Does she feel smaller? Does she feel bigger? Is she filled with guilt or relief from guilt? Does she tend to be filled with remorse or motivation? What kind of outcome tends to flow from her raised awareness of the Holy in her life? How?

This attention to the Holy has a long history among pastoral care givers, but as chaplains we have usually made assumptions about its role and function rather than inquiring. We know that we are "living reminders" of one greater than ourselves, of God or the Holy. We have tended to assume that we knew what that meant to people. Most often we believed it meant what it meant to us. As we built *The Discipline,* we began to better understand we could not make that assumption. If we were living reminders, we needed to know the content of that reminder and the difference it made in the individual patient's life in this health crisis. Since we were a reminder, whether we liked it or not, it was necessary to learn what kind of impact we were having simply by showing up.

FIGURE 4

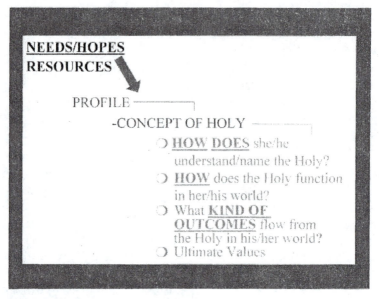

NEEDS/HOPES
RESOURCES

PROFILE
-CONCEPT OF HOLY
○ **HOW DOES** she/he
understand/name the Holy?
○ **HOW** does the Holy function
in her/his world?
○ What **KIND OF**
OUTCOMES flow from
the Holy in his/her world?
○ Ultimate Values

© Chaplain Arthur M. Lucas. Reprinted with permission.

Chaplains have known for a long time that they represent something far larger than themselves, something granted them by the patient as a given part of an identity in the relationship. We are now clearer that this representation for the individual patient provides information concerning the role and function of the Holy and how it functions in life. It is this function we want to engage for healing and well-being. Our job is to engage and help the person better engage the extant spirituality there. Rather than assume or correct it, we are to raise and deal with issues that patients are experiencing, beginning with the very dynamics and functions of spirituality rather than matters of categorization.

Meaning

In this component we posit most of the usual material concerning identity, purpose, direction, sense of personhood, and role in the world. Our emphasis is on how and where patients find meaning (Figure 5). It is especially important to learn how the current health challenge threatens or in some other way challenges and/or changes that sense of meaning.

FIGURE 5

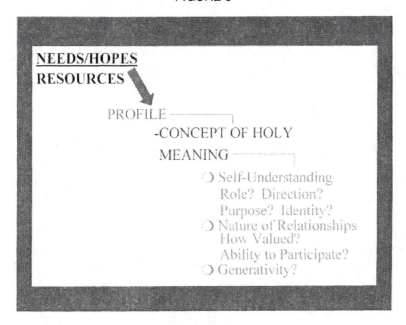

We attend to the meaning rather than the shape through which it is expressed, the substance rather than the form it might take. For example, a young woman under our care presented with a combination of health problems that resulted in, among other things, a chronic neurologic limitation. Her fine, small motor skills were impaired, something many of us probably would not notice a year or two after its onset. In her case, however, it made a big difference because she was a guitarist. She had understood that she had purpose and worth because she "created beauty in the world" by playing her guitar. If she could not play the guitar, she doubted that she had any place in the world, that she would even understand herself. The chaplain helped her work through this crisis by getting down to the substance of the concern, namely *how* to create beauty in the world. It turned out the guitar was a means to an end, not the meaning itself. The patient's hobby was painting, at which she was quite good. Her painting was a way of creating beauty in the world as well and her ability to paint was not affected by her particular fine motor skill impairment. With this insight and resource, she entertained the possibility that there would be meaning for her in the world, in fact the same meaning through different means. The patient was then able to engage her own healing, participating in her own rehabilitation and aftercare. Rather than just getting her to be compliant, the chaplain's ministry gave the patient a sense of ownership, participation and role in her own healing and well-being. And that, cumulatively, made all the subsequent difference in her excellent recovery.

Another dimension is how participation in making meaning might help deal with illnesses. Some persons have a sense of meaning in being able to assert themselves and cope with whatever is before them, handling it themselves as much as they can. When such persons become ill, they will continue to pursue meaning in the health care environment in the same way, even through everyone is trying to do "for" her, to take care of her needs. Sometimes, as many chaplains have observed, it is actually this source of meaning and purpose that is at the root of conflicts between patients and their health care teams. The team members are doing something for her that she could do for herself, and that she would find meaning in doing. Looking at such situations from the vantage point of meaning takes them out of the context of power struggles and interprets them in ways particular to the patient's life. That kind of paradigm shift, faithful to the patient's values, is a type of contribution we can make from a spiritual care perspective.

Hope

The *Hope* component contains at least two layers (Figure 6). One layer with which many are already familiar concerns the individual's hope as "ultimate" and "intermediate." An ultimate hope is over-arching and independent of whatever happens in the moment. Examples may include a patient's belief that even if she dies due to this illness, she will go to heaven. An intermediate hope, while potentially attainable, is vulnerable to the course of the illness or treatment. For instance a patient may hope to go to a cousin's wedding even though the cancer threatens to take her life shortly.

Ultimate or intermediate hopes can serve the patient's ability to cope and live a meaningful, changed life. Knowing which sort of hope is serving this patient allows the chaplain to engage it in helpful ways for her well-being. Hope can provide energy, resources for living,

FIGURE 6

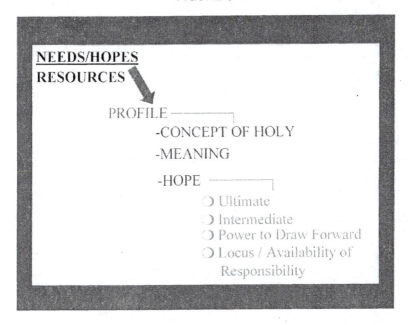

NEEDS/HOPES
RESOURCES

PROFILE
-CONCEPT OF HOLY
-MEANING
-HOPE
) Ultimate
) Intermediate
) Power to Draw Forward
) Locus / Availability of
Responsibility

healing, and well-being–even incorporating a disease experience. It can help her lean forward into living rather than settling for being a patient.

Another part of hope is its locus of responsibility and availability. Is it something within which she has ownership? Is there a role she has to play in order to see things through to the hope? Or is it something she simply counts on from others? Is all the hope "out there" in medical science, or God, or caregivers or "the kindness of others?" Is the locus a combination that lends itself to partnership between herself and those providing care or others? Does her hoping even lend itself to partnership or is it always pointed toward autonomy or toward dependence? We do not experience any one of these as generically right or wrong. How do we best "match up" to her hoping to engage it best? Remember, that is our purpose; it is to engage her hope(s), and communicate it so others can also engage it for the well-being of this person.

Community

In this fourth component, we first clarify for ourselves whether the patient has a functioning sense of community at all (Figure 7). Having people around does not equal community. How do we know if the people around this patient function as a community? Even once we know that, it is important to know how this community functions in her life. While people are often nurtured by a community that still leaves open the impact and nature of that nurturance. Is it positive, negative, or nil? Care must be taken to avoid projective assumptions. Negative nurture can come from forms of community we expect or assume will be positive. Once again chaplains must focus on dynamic function and substance rather than on form and appearance in order to emphasize the active, relational aspects for care.

For instance, imagine that a patient is facing his alcoholism for the first time, owning up to it and trying to do something constructive about it. He may not want to hear from the church in which he has been a leader and in which alcoholism marks a person as a sinner. He

FIGURE 7

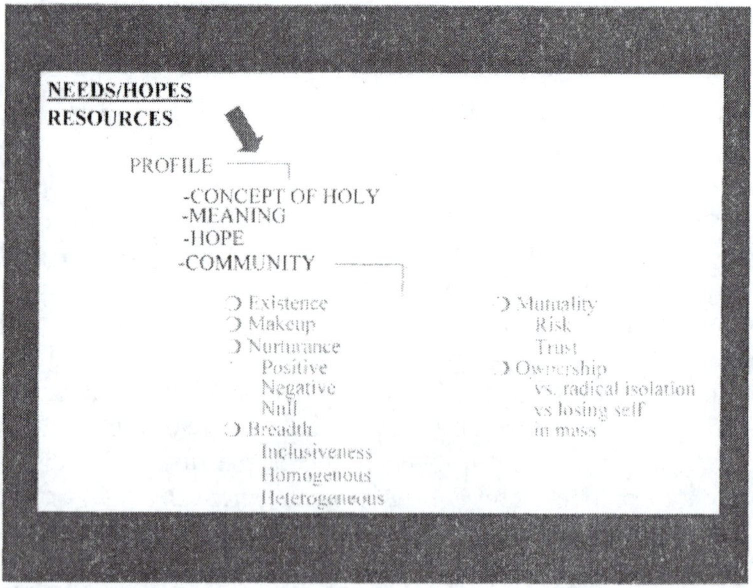

© Chaplain Arthur M. Lucas. Reprinted with permission.

may not want to give up the esteem or role he enjoys in the faith community. He may fear facing the implications for himself of the theology he has embraced. To encourage the community to visit, or even thinking about the church community, may yield a negative nurturance. This is important for us to know if our primary investment is in his healing and well-being. It might lead to some different kind of consultation with the clergy person who does know about the admission. It might lead to a different sort of plan about how we manage visitation. It might form part of our plan to explore the theology with which he lives. It has an important impact on the patient and it is something that needs to be a part of our profile.

Another part of community is the importance of observing whether the community tends to be homogenous or heterogeneous. Our simple observation over time, untested by research, is that, given the same clinical context, more homogenous communities tend to offer fewer resources. These homogenous communities tend to be very similar to the patient. We observe that more heterogeneous communities tend to provide more variety or breadth of resources to their members and this bodes well for recovery. We can only hypothesize that this has something to do with a wider variety of resources available to him within community. This merits further systematic attention in the future.

The next element of community concerns mutuality. Is there an ability to take risks within the community or is everything a risk of community? Is there a sense of trust in the community? If so, how transferable is it? Is the person able to form a trusting community with caregivers? Later in this volume, one of our chaplains will describe the capacity to trust as a major predictor of whether lung transplant patients recover well. Dynamically, it seems not to matter who patients trust, God, the surgeon, the chaplain, the hospital, the city . . . It's the capacity for trust in relationship (or community) that seems to make a difference. Not surprisingly, therefore, this chaplain quickly begins looking for this capacity to trust among lung transplant patients.

What sort of role does the patient play in his community? Giver? Receiver? Authority? Neophyte? Leader? Follower? Constant? Occasional? How flexible is the patient between these roles and more? Does he radically individuate himself, aggressively asserting his place outside any community available to him, negating any sense of connected personhood? Does he lose his individual identity to and into the community, becoming nothing apart from his being with the community? This is all information about what is missing in the rarified isolation of hospitalization, a very real need. It is also information about the roles patients can play in their own care. The results of our assessment suggest whether we may need to complement or surrogate some of these roles in our care plan.

Desired Contributing Outcomes

The next step in *The Discipline* is to have some idea what difference we hope and intend our ministry will make for the healing and well being of the person in our care. What are the "desired contributing outcomes"? (See Figure 8.) Originally, much of our work started with attention to outcomes because we believed they were more important than simply the "being" of the caregiver in and of itself.

One of our initial questions concerned whether caring was really about us, the caregivers. Was it about our being a caring presence or was it about the impact of our caring presence on the patient? We have concluded that, as chaplains, caring ultimately and definitively is not

FIGURE 8

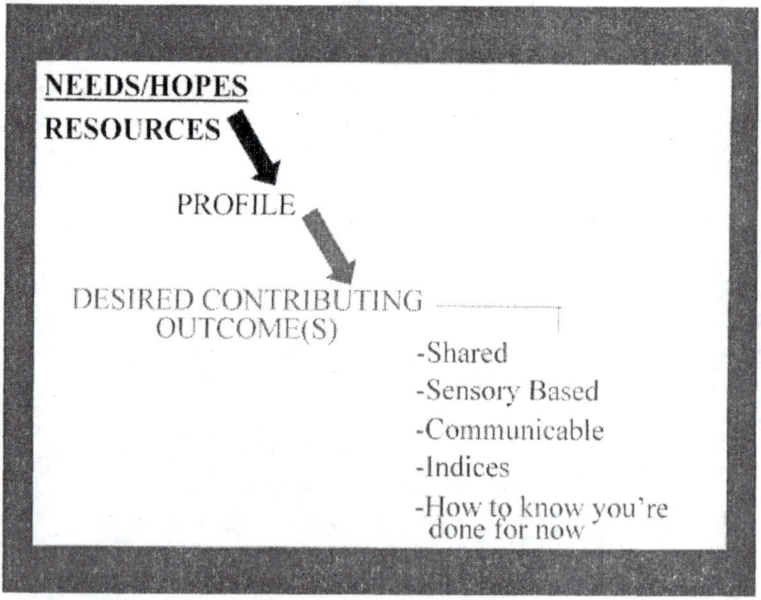

NEEDS/HOPES
RESOURCES
        PROFILE

DESIRED CONTRIBUTING
        OUTCOME(S)
                -Shared
                -Sensory Based
                -Communicable
                -Indices
                -How to know you're
                done for now

about us. It is about the person(s) in our care. If we expect our caring presence to benefit them, then we are concerned about outcomes, whatever we call them.

We found it important to make a distinction between "activity" and "outcome." An activity is something the chaplain can be or can do. Examples include being fully present, being vulnerable, being available, active listening, praying, inviting, reflecting, or confronting. An outcome is what impact or difference these activities make. Examples include the patient's lowered anxiety, increased hope, knowing she is not alone, ownership for her well-being, or feeling empowered. Activities are about the caregiver. Outcomes are about the effect of those activities, for good or ill, with the patient. Nor is it about the effect intended; rather, it is about the effect experienced by the patient.

A well-formed outcome is sensory-based, can be communicated, and is shared.

- *Sensory-based*: It can be expressed to others and recognized when it happens in terms of what we see, hear and feel. Rather than simply asserting that the patient's sadness will lift, we can say the patient will improve in maintaining eye contact, show more variation in the tone of his speech, and show more interest in what is happening around him.
- *Communicable*: It can be briefly described to other members of the team in terms that have meaning for their perception of how this outcome fits within the over-all interdisciplinary care plan and objectives. Our rule of thumb: when the chaplain's description of the desired contributing outcome requires a second sentence, it is time to ask whether it is sufficiently clear for others as they try to hear or read it.
- *Shared*: It is shared with the person for whom we are providing care. This may or may not mean a formal contract as in pastoral counseling, but it does mean that, through the pastoral dialogue, patients own the desirability and definition of the intended outcome along with the chaplain. It is not just the projective, imagined, or idealized plan of the chaplain. It is also a direction, a wish, hope, dream, or desired outcome of the person in our care. It's ours together with the patient.

When we started using the word "outcome" we were a little put off because we automatically thought all outcomes were like wound healing, shortening lengths of stay, or reducing resource utilization. We asked ourselves, "After we have gotten to know the patient, what are we hoping for? What is our prayer for the patient?" Then we could more easily own all those good things for which we hoped and prayed, thinking of them as desired outcomes. We could define and own spiritual outcomes uniquely available to individual patients and know that they contributed to outcomes desired by the team, e.g., a recovery or appropriate death or not having to come back to the hospital for this cause.

What are *our* contributing outcomes? How are they uniquely spiritual? How do we define and contextualize them? How can that be done in the case-by-case care of patients and in the larger context of health care? Defining our contributions out of a ministry of presence, relationship, process, dialogue, knowledge, and faith continues to be hard work. It entails helping people from other disciplines understand how our contributions are important for healing and well-being. For instance, assume that a patient suffers from being isolated from her familiar relationships during this hospital experience. A perfectly good pastoral contributing outcome is to help her realize that she has a "friend at her side" in the person of the chaplain, that someone cares about her, and that she is truly heard and supported. We need to be able to integrate this outcome with the other contributing outcomes from the team. This ministry can make a legitimate contribution, as legitimate a contributing outcome as "infection free" or "O_2 level increased." Given our spiritual assessment, we have reason to expect she will bring more valuable personal resources to her own healing as her sense of isolation diminishes. This outcome of "experiencing relationship" is very similar to "lessening pain." It is a perfectly good contributing outcome that adds to the patient's healing and well-being.

A contributing outcome must be well-formed so that we know when we are done for now. We cannot know when we are done if our contributing outcome is not sensory-based and clear enough for us to communicate to others. If we need more than three sentences to describe and contextualize an outcome, it is not yet well-formed. If it is not clear enough in our heads, we cannot know when we are done, we cannot know how to move toward it, we cannot know how to communicate it with others, and we cannot be sure it contributes to the whole. Figure 9 lists a few of the recurrent desired contributing outcomes our chaplains have experienced as important in everyday clinical settings.

FIGURE 9. Examples of Desired Contributing Outcomes

CABG Surgery Patients: Chaplain Robert Yim

- Patient perceives self as subject rather than object, capable of being an agent in his/her own care
- Patient's idea of success is reformulated to incorporate the present situation, but does not overwhelm his/her
- Patient is willing to explore what other meanings life can have for his/her

Lung Transplant Patients: Chaplain Cheryl Palmer

- Patient able to engage trust as a resource
- Patient/support person(s) able to verbalize the significance of his/her transplant to life goals, beliefs, values, significant relationships and religious practices

Oncology Patients: Chaplain Julie Allen Berger

- **At diagnosis:** Patient/loved ones can identify spiritual questions raised by shock of diagnosis and specific spiritual resources to help with coping
- **Response to treatment:** Patient/loved ones can recognize a continuum of hope and identify how life projects/goals are re-prioritized by cancer experience
- **Moving on into life/preparing for death:** Patient/loved ones reappraise spirituality and coping skills in preparation for future challenges

Breast Cancer Patients: Chaplain Linda Horrell

- Patient is able to identify hope(s), both intermediate and ultimate
- Patient identifies and makes use of others to dialogue about gender and feminine identity

Acute Psychiatry Patients: Chaplain Fred Smoot

- Patient able to recall acts of caring done both by the patient and for him/her

Geriatric Psychiatry Patients: Chaplain Fred Smoot

- Renewed confidence and integrity involving faith/religious life histories through remembering and life review

Stroke Patients: Chaplain Lisa ScottJointer

- Patient/family motivated to reassess locus of control and explore new approaches to their ways of relating in community, family, faith traditions, and with self

Rehabilitation Patients: Chaplain Lisa ScottJointer

- Patient/family understand how disability integrates with spiritual values in life
- Patient/family able to re-integrate into life style and utilize spiritual values for support

Intensive Care Patients: Chaplain Linda Horrell

- Recovering patient is able to identify good reasons for improving medical self-understanding, for self-care
- Patient facing end-of-life is able to grieve and make meaning of the end-of-life

Plan

We must create a plan once we grasp the Needs, Hopes and Resources of the person, formulate a spiritual profile, and define contributing outcomes. What is the plan for spiritual care and how does it integrate with the overall care plan? (See Figure 10.)

The plan must be clear and communicable. A good plan requires distinct definition of responsibilities. A well-formed plan will, in so far as possible, draw on the resources of the person to whom we are providing care. And delivering the desired contributing outcome cannot simply be the chaplain's responsibility without involvement of the patient. In the above example of the isolated patient, we intend opportunities for her to experience relationship so as to enable her inner resources. She, however, has to be open to attending to our presence. She needs to have at least some sense of availability and safety to experience the opportunity. She must take some risks of her own or else our being there day and night is not going to communi-

FIGURE 10

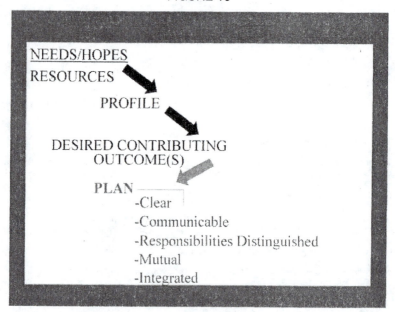

© Chaplain Arthur M. Lucas. Reprinted with permission.

cate anything about relationship. If she does not live up to her role, we can play ours perfectly and contribute no outcome. There is a simple mutuality in a good plan. We communicate respect for the patient through that and we avoid unnecessarily running ourselves into the ground.

This brings us to the main reason for having indices, markers of progress (or lack of progress) along the way toward a desired outcome. They give the chaplain a chance for course adjustment rather than a pass/fail at the end. Even if all are playing their parts in the plan, it may not function as intended. The indices make it clear when the plan is working and when it is not working. The indices may tell us that the identified contributing outcome is a wrong one, or maybe one of the participants is not doing his part. If we are not clear about the mutuality and responsibilities involved in the plan, the caregiver may be adrift, trying to figure out what is going wrong. We cannot know unless we are clear about the plan, are clear about distinct responsibilities in the plan, and have indices along the way to measure the desired contributing outcomes.

And the plan must be integrated within the whole interdisciplinary care plan for this patient/family. How does the spiritual care plan complement or conflict with elements of the rest of the team's care plan? For example, perhaps the spiritual care plan emphasizes quiet, meditative reflection with journaling about her experience at significant points throughout her waking hours and sharing these with the chaplain. The other care plans, however, may fill the patient's day with physical rehabilitation activities at the end of which the patient is completely exhausted. Or again, the spiritual care dimension of the plan may focus on the patient's ownership of her role in her own healing and well-being. In contrast, the plans of other team members involve her in intensive educational efforts. Conflict and confusion will result. Even if JCAHO never visited again and never again looked at a chart to assess the integration of interdisciplinary care plans, the best thing for the patient's healing and well-being is that the interventions and intentions of all those providing her care are thoughtfully integrated with each other and with the patient.

Interventions

Once the patient and the chaplain have a plan, we bring it to life. The things we intentionally do in the name of movement toward contributing desired outcomes constitute interventions (Figure 11). Interventions include being with the patient in the ways we believe will be helpful. Interventions include doing what we planned, in the way we assessed would be helpful and with an eye toward the contributions to care we intended to make. Spiritual care interventions are characterized by presence and absence and a nonjudgmental relationship. They are, at base, relational, intentional and something for which we own responsibility. And they are faithful.

Faithfulness relates to our interventions from many angles. It pertains to carrying out the plan, but it also means being faithful to the beliefs, values, and commitments of patients. Additionally, it requires faithfulness to our own values with the ability to facilitate good care for the person. Finally, we need to be faithful in the continuity of care, providing service as seamlessly as possible across providers.

Interventions can range from questions to confrontation to prayer to silent hand holding to reading scripture to active listening to personal sharing and everything in between. Pastoral interventions are well

FIGURE 11

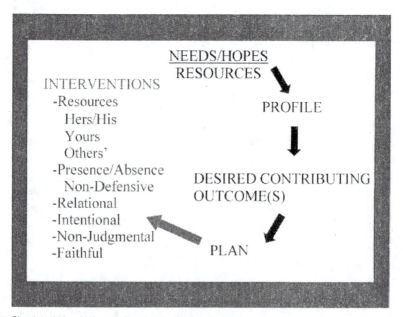

© Chaplain Arthur M. Lucas. Reprinted with permission.

known and need not be described here at length. Applying *The Discipline* does not explicitly change the availability or appropriateness of any of these behaviors, but it does raise our consciousness and intentionality. In doing so, it blunts tendencies to "do what we always do" and keeps us focused on our carefully considered activities contributing patient outcomes that are understood by the team and shared with the patient.

Measurement

Then comes measurement; worthwhile and scary (Figure 12). The referents for measurement are the desired contributing outcomes we defined. Spiritual care providers are so accustomed to picking up on what's going on right now and imagining what's next. We so often overlook what was, the distance we have come, that on which the "now" is based. This "overlooking" leads to a lot of unnecessary anxiety, unappreciated contributions, and a whole lot of extra work. For the measurement stage, it is important to look back on how the

FIGURE 12

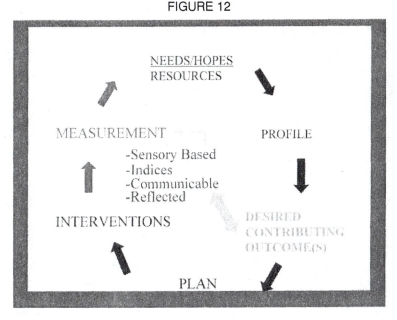

NEEDS/HOPES
RESOURCES

PROFILE

MEASUREMENT
-Sensory Based
-Indices
-Communicable
-Reflected

INTERVENTIONS

DESIRED
CONTRIBUTING
OUTCOME(S)

PLAN

chaplain and the patient/family have done against the agreed upon outcomes, not new challenges in front of us.

The measurements need to be sensory-based, just like we defined the desired contributing outcome(s). Pay attention to the indices laid out earlier in defining the outcomes of ministry. Be able to communicate the measures and reflect on them.

Imagine how that can be important. Imagine a hospitalized patient who is isolated from a home community in which she experiences meaning and which positively nurtured her sense of worth and ability. She misses this and it shows in her sadness and her lack of personal resourcefulness for coping with the challenges of her illness and treatment. We hope she experiences the chaplain's presence as caring in much the same way she experiences her home community. To bring that plan to life, the chaplain plans to visit in certain ways and times. The chaplain accomplishes that. And here the chaplain is, three days after that initial time together, visiting her in the morning on the day of discharge. As the visit begins, she picks up the conversation by sharing in a spontaneous and trusting manner how glad she is she's doing better, but she's really anxious right now because she has come to count so much on the attentive, compassionate care provided by the nurses, the doctors, and her chaplain. She is not sure at all if she can go home and feel as safe and cared for as here, much less be able to take care of herself in a way that her healing will continue. Yes, her niece is coming. And yes, home health is arranged. She's met the home health nurse and she's looking forward to seeing her at home. Her anxiety is well based given the intensity of the illness, the care she has experienced, the rapidity with which she is being discharged, and the amount of care and self-care still before her. If the chaplain tries to measure the effectiveness of the care without referring back to where the relationship began, no one will have a sense of what was contributed.

By referencing back to the initial assessment three days ago and the desired contributing outcomes, the chaplain might say to her:

> Mrs. X, I hear your anxiety and I think I can understand it given what you've been through and what you are facing as you go home. I want to talk with you about that in just a minute. Before I do, I want to let you know I noticed something. Do you remember when I first met you and we talked about how isolated you

felt and your sense of being out of community, in fact out of community with God? And now here you are just a few days later talking to me about how close you've become to the people who've been providing your care, including me. How much you're looking forward to your niece being here tomorrow and that home health care nurse. Do you realize how connected to folks you are able to feel when just a little while ago, not only were you suffering because of the lack of that, you weren't even sure you could manage it anymore with God or anyone else? I hope you realize how far you've come and that you can connect to folks just fine.

If the chaplain is not organized enough (I know that sounds mundane), and does not have the courage (that is not mundane) to look back on goals set, we can never make an intervention like that. All we could do is think about what's next and then usually feel inadequate because we had not done enough.

If chaplains are clear about their desired contributing outcomes, about measuring against them even when they are not realized, then it is equally clear about what had not happened. This clarity creates or strengthens a mechanism to reassess and reflect. If chaplains are clear about desired contributing outcomes, about measuring against them and reaching some of them, then s/he can think not only about what has not been done but also about what has been accomplished, during the trip home in the evening. It is then easier to leave the patients and go home in peace, claiming a sort of harmony that encourages the chaplain to come back the next day. Applying *The Discipline,* along with some courage, helps chaplains serve not only Mrs. X but also their own well-being.

Overview

When we take an overview of this discipline, the right side of the cycle includes the Profile and the Desired Contributing Outcomes in which the primary function is assessing (Figure 13). And we need to realize that even as we go about assessing, we are effectively giving pastoral care. In other words, even when we seem to be only assessing, we are *intervening* and must do so with intentionality. That side of the cycle emphasizes assessment, and we must be mindful that interventions are going on simultaneously, interventions that are making a difference. If we think we are only getting to know the patient/family, we will leave to chance the outcomes we are already facilitating as well as whether those outcomes are either desired or contribute to the healing and well-being of the person in our care.

The left side of *The Discipline* is primarily interventional (Figure 14). The mix in the pastoral relationship and focus is high on the pastoral intervention but we must also pay attention to gathering new information, getting to know the patient/family in deeper ways, and refining our profile and plan. So even when the emphasis is on intervention, we are also assessing. It is always a mix for spiritual care professionals because of the nature of the dimensions to which we give attention and the inherently intense, relational nature of our most effective means. Even good surgeons continue to evaluate their patient after the incision is made and the interventions for good coronary artery bypass surgery have begun. However, the nature of the interventional and assessment activities is easily distinct. For chaplains, the distinctiveness of the two is more difficult to perceive because our

FIGURE 13

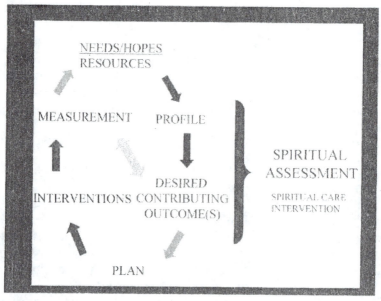

"person" is the primary "tool" in both intervening and assessing. The point of the awareness on this side of *The Discipline* is to remember to continue attending and learning even while consciously intervening in ways appropriate to the desired contributing outcome and within the plan of spiritual care. So often chaplains feel like they must either be attending to the patient or "doing something." We need to keep reminding ourselves the two are far from mutually exclusive. They are always both/and intertwined with each other in our pastoral relationships.

In fact, *The Discipline* is a mix of these cycles. In complex patient and family relationships, we may be at different points in *The Discipline* for each of the important dynamics in the care giving relationship. If we have a discipline for what we are about, we can sort those out. We can know where we are and where we stand and how to move from where we are to whatever is next for the patient's well-being. We can be accountable for our ministry, we can assert our authority, and we can integrate our care into the patient's overall plan.

FIGURE 14

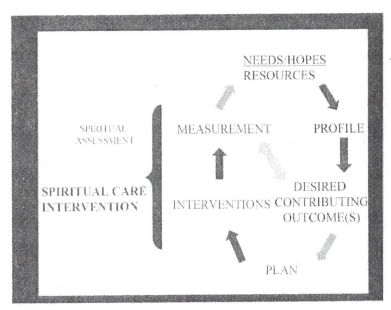

© Chaplain Arthur M. Lucas. Reprinted with permission.

OTHER EFFECTS OF THE DISCIPLINE

Patient Satisfaction and Experienced Contributions

The Discipline enabled us to maintain and improve the satisfaction of patients and family members under our care. We used the *Patient Satisfaction Instrument for Pastoral Care*[3] and its results suggested that we were consistently relevant to patient concerns, i.e., readiness to go home, healing and being cared for. This was all the more important as the length-of-stay shortened and opportunities for return contacts shrank. When we looked at the results from this instrument, they showed that, on the average, our chaplains saw a given patient fewer times than chaplains in other hospitals. However, we gained the same level of satisfaction and we tended to be more consistently relevant to patient concerns, all with fewer visits. These results suggested that *The Discipline* was useful even in a setting where we were making fewer visits and still maintaining our effectiveness in terms of patient satisfaction.

Department and Services

As we more consistently applied *The Discipline* in our pastoral practice some changes occurred relative to our department.

- Expectations went up. Fast! Other professionals were clearer about how we could help and quickly called on us increasingly.
- We have gone from mostly driven by emergent/urgent calls to mostly driven by regular care responsibilities. That has necessitated PRN staffing to cover pastoral responsibilities when chaplains are on vacation.
- We have had to give up our mysterious, good-guy image.
- We have markedly fewer friendly visits, especially follow-up friendly-only contacts. Patients are more likely to take the initiative to pick up on a conversation where it was left off.

The scope and nature of our referrals changed when we implemented *The Discipline*. Before implementation, we consistently received calls (to which we were to respond immediately) for sacramental needs of Catholic patients. Since implementation, we are also called for all Level 1 Traumas, all deaths (for which we provide bereavement care and approach the family regarding tissue/organ donation), all cardio-pulmonary resuscitations (CPR's), and all employee deaths. We are notified of all admissions for heart catheterizations, coronary artery bypass graft surgeries, lung transplants, volume reduction surgeries, cystic fibrosis admissions, bone marrow transplants, liver transplants, kidney transplants, islet cell transplants, victim of violence admissions, strokes, and vent dependent care. We are notified of the implementation of terminal wean and brain death protocol implementations, implementation of Do-Not-Resuscitate status, and end of life care.

The range of services we offer has also changed. Before implementing this model, our services consisted of basic direct patient/family care, worship provision, sacramental care and a little staff support. Since implementation, that list has grown in response to the increasing variety of demands for our care and we receive opportunities for participation in the larger scope of the hospital. Of course, the core of the original elements remains, but even they are different in depth and character now.

Research

Now we know how laborious and time-consuming substantive research is. We believe it is impossible to conduct spiritual care research without constructing some model by which care is standardized at some level. *The Discipline* provides that groundwork. A consistent process and language is necessary in order to see patterns that lead to hypotheses and the testing process.

Without being able to identify contributing outcomes and discreet interventions toward outcomes, clinical research would be more impossible than laborious. Now we can clarify ideas about hypotheses and embrace what we now call "Development and Research" as a part of our departmental mission in this quaternary, research, teaching hospital. We have been able to take the first, excruciatingly small steps into doing research and learn from the good pastoral care research done by others.

Clinical Pastoral Education

Association for Clinical Pastoral Education accredited programming has long been an integral part of spiritual care at Barnes-Jewish. As we integrated an outcome orientation and *The Discipline* into our departmental care, we realized its incongruence with the pastoral perspective we taught and nurtured in our CPE program. We identified the changes that could be made while maintaining key CPE character-istics and processes, much like we moved into assessments and out-comes orientation while maintaining the characteristics and strengths of pastoral care. Our CPE programs now starts by introducing an outcome orientation for spiritual care giving. The introduction of *The Discipline* early in CPE interns' and residents' training provides them a common language for the struggles about personal availability, pas-toral presence and identity, authority, professionalism, and role differ-entiation without obviating the struggles themselves. Students who come from other CPE programs report that *The Discipline* contributes to group formation and engagement, primarily through quickly introducing a common way to engage common struggles.

We were concerned that introducing *The Discipline* would result in "cookie cutter" care givers being churned out by the program, rob-bing the students of the burden and opportunity to discover their own care giving as it emerged in the process. Within some limits, this fear has been assuaged. The students are thoroughly oriented to pastoral outcomes when they emerge from the program. How they bring that orientation to life remains as much a discovery and creation for them as before. More specifically, in a residency unit that included students from other centers, ours had an easier time identifying their own spiritual assessment models. While the other students tended to adopt or reject the models we studied, our residents were more able to adapt, reconstruct, or "be different from" *The Discipline* in ways faithfully expressive of their gifts for, experience with, and insights into spiritual care. Further discussion on *The Discipline* and CPE are found later in this volume.

CONCLUSION

Creating and developing *The Discipline* has made a difference in our care. We have risked much and learned a lot. It has resulted in the interdisciplinary integration of our care in accountable ways and in-creased our contributions to patients and families.

The Discipline requires further development and research. For instance we have developed customized models more immediately specific for heart, oncology, thoracic trauma, and HIV/AIDS patients. We are working on customization for neurology and psychiatry pa-tients. And we have begun research with victims of violence, women living with HIV/AIDS, and others. Some of these are described in the materials that follow. *The Discipline* is proving to be a demanding and sound infrastructure that promotes integrated and accountable service, faithful to the heart and core of pastoral care giving

NOTES

1. In identifying these foci, we were inspired by the system developed at Mt. Carmel Medical Center in Columbus, Ohio.

2. It must be acknowledged that most of us long ago studied Paul Pruyser's *Minister as Diagnostician*, James Lapsley's *Salvation and Health,* and spiritual development works by Kohler, Fowler, and others. While we acknowledge the influence that these works undoubtedly had on our development, none were specifically used in our explication of our four foci.

3. See: VandeCreek, L. (1997). Ministry of hospital chaplains: Patient Satisfaction. *Journal of Health Care Chaplaincy,* 6(2), 1-61.

A Case Study:
Linda

Julie Allen Berger, DMin, BCC

SUMMARY. An oncology chaplain illustrates *The Discipline for Pastoral Care Giving* by recalling interactions with a breast cancer patient.

KEYWORDS. Oncology chaplain, Discipline for Pastoral Care Giving, outcome-oriented chaplaincy, spiritual assessment, breast cancer

We will call her "Linda," a woman in her forties from a small town 3 hours away from our treatment center and newly diagnosed with advanced stage breast cancer. She came into our spiritual care office anxious and crying on the first day her chemotherapy was scheduled (Figure 1). "Will you come to the treatment room with me and my husband?" She was afraid and thrown off her emotional balance, sure that there was no room in her life plans to leave her family prematurely.

She was a mother of young adult children, a wife, and employed at

Rev. Julie Allen Berger is Chaplain for Oncology Services, Barnes-Jewish Hospital at Washington University Medical Center, St. Louis, MO 63110 (E-mail: jab0539@bjc.org).

FIGURE 1. Linda: Needs/Hopes/Resources

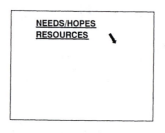

- Need: "Not sure I can tolerate this chemo."

- Hope: "I want to survive this cancer."

- Resources: "I have my family, faith, church (but not my pastor)."

© Julie Allen Berger. Reprinted with permission.

her home church as a secretary. Her pastor/employer/friend had recently moved to a new congregation in another state.

In exploring Linda's feelings on this first visit, this profile emerged (Figure 2):

- Her *concept of the holy* was of a God who would reward her with good health if she were a dutiful, upbeat cancer patient.
- She struggled with the *meaning* of her illness as she questioned how this cancer could happen to her, a healthy woman with good genes.
- Her strong *hope* was to see through her roles as mother and grandmother and wife. The vision of grandchildren yet to be born pulled her forward through her first treatment day anxieties and lots of other up's and down's in her journey with cancer.
- She experienced good support from family and congregation and neighbors, but her pastor's departure and her husband's job as a truck driver were real concerns for her as she took stock of who her community would be. I think this is part of why she sought the chaplain out, first thing.

It wasn't hard to come up with a *desired contributing outcome* on that first meeting with Linda and her husband (Figure 3). She was so jumpy and jittery getting started with her chemo that her nurse didn't

FIGURE 2. Linda: Profile

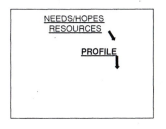

- "God helps those who help themselves."

- "No one in our family has ever had cancer."

- "I want to see my grandchildren."

- "Our family is strong, but my husband drives a truck and my girls are just starting out in life."

FIGURE 3. Linda: Desired Contributing Outcome

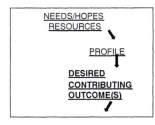

- As Linda feels calmer, she'll be able to recall/draw upon spiritual strengths.

even try to finish going over potential side effects with her. He gave the handout to her husband saying, "You two read this later at home."

Between her cancer diagnosis and losing her pastor, Linda felt the rug pulled out from under her, with the sense that her spiritual guide was not there at a critical time. I know, and I think Linda's husband realized, that Linda had a relationship with God that was not totally dependent on the pastor. We worked on reminding Linda that she was not alone.

The oncology staff worked well as a team in Linda's case. For several of us on the team (the social worker, RN and myself), lowering

Linda's anxiety was going to be crucial to her ability to cope (Figure 4). Linda was given names of counselors in her local community by the social worker, and Linda and I wondered together how she could build in a sense that she had a local "pastor" she could talk to about her spiritual struggles since diagnosis. I know that Linda's husband encouraged her to follow through on these suggestions . . . the team wondered if she could get it together to act on them.

In my first visit with Linda, and in subsequent conversations, talking about all the sudden losses she'd been asked to weather was helpful (Figure 5). She'd temporarily lost her health, sense of certainty about the future, spiritual leader, boss.

She needed to talk about all the life plans that were now thrown

FIGURE 4. Linda: Plan/Integration

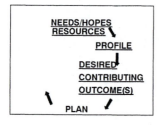

- Decrease anxiety.

- Connect with spiritual/ mental health resources.

FIGURE 5. Linda: Interventions

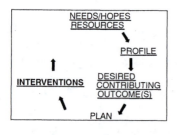

- Explore losses with chaplain.

- Locate local pastor for support.

- Create new "future story."

open to question: would she get to ripen with her husband into older age and retirement? Would she see her daughters marry and have families of their own? Andrew Lester's (1995) concept of "future story" is a good one here. Linda needed to mourn ways her future might be different from what she'd always imagined, and find a way to build a revised story.

Did the chaplain's plan and interventions help decrease Linda's anxiety? It seemed to, witnessed by Linda's unprompted reports back on her next visit to the clinic (Figure 6). She told me proudly about making it through her first round of chemotherapy and its side effects. She, on her own, had searched out another Protestant woman minister in her town, and initiated weekly meetings with her. She also began seeing a local counselor. The whole team was thrilled and relieved to see that Linda's anxiety was not as crippling as we'd feared.

Linda reported that the cancer process remained frightening for her, but that she had regained a sense that God was with her in this experience, giving what she needed to get through it. She gave us her own measurement.

Linda and her family were able to cope pretty well with the trips back and forth to St. Louis for treatment, buoyed by the hope that her chemo was knocking out her cancer. The anxiety Linda experienced, on learning that cancer was still present after treatment, was just as

FIGURE 6. Linda: Measurement

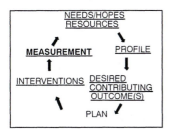

- "I feel like I can hang in there a day at a time."

- "I found a woman pastor at home to talk to."

- "I've been able to pray. Even though I'm still afraid, God gives me peace."

high as at the time of diagnosis. But now her anger surfaced as well . . . at God, at herself for daring to hope, at the chemotherapy for letting her down (Figure 7). One of her most important resources, her relationship with God, presently felt shaky.

The place in Linda's spiritual profile that really stood out now was her rage at God (Figure 8). Fortunately, the pastor she was seeing at home had really helped Linda articulate the outrage and betrayal she felt towards God. When I would see Linda in clinic, she was honest about her struggles to believe that God was still "on her side," or even listening to her at all. She wrestled, too, with the *meaning* of her treatment failure: what was the purpose of all that hard work in chemo if the cancer didn't budge?

At this point in my relationship with Linda, serving as a reminder of God's presence in the midst of adversity seemed to be my primary role

FIGURE 7. Linda: Next Critical Juncture–Needs/Hopes/Resources

- "Chemo failed. My cancer grew."

- "I'm scared and angry."

© Julie Allen Berger. Reprinted with permission.

FIGURE 8. Linda: Next Critical Juncture–Profile

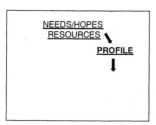

- "God, I kept my end of the bargain. You failed me."

© Julie Allen Berger. Reprinted with permission.

as chaplain (Figure 9). This is a desired contributing outcome many of us strive for consciously or unconsciously with our patients all the time.

Though we didn't ever speak by phone, it was clear from what Linda was reporting to me, that her newfound pastor friend and I were hoping for similar things for Linda in the way of outcomes contributing towards her health.

The concrete plan Linda and I agreed upon was that, at her request, the nurse would page me when she came for more chemo or radiation (Figure 10). I like that the plan was mutual, and gave Linda some sense of ownership: she had the choice to call, or not. Later on in Linda's journey with cancer, when her physicians knew they were going to be sharing more bad news with Linda and her husband, they would page me to "be on the ready" to offer spiritual care to the couple after their conferences with them. Sometimes the staff wanted spiritual care, too.

It doesn't always happen this way, but in Linda's case, the medical oncology team worked well as an integrated whole. We anticipated and responded to Linda's emerging needs and hopes, recognizing as well her sizeable resources in coping despite her anxiety.

As I mentioned, Linda's local pastor and I were practicing parallel interventions in encouraging Linda to put into words and prayer her bewilderment and frustration with God (Figure 11). As Linda was able to do this, I noted with her the strength I observed in her sense of righteous indignation. I noted her strengths as a survivor of cancer for a year. I wondered with her if there were ways God had helped her, or stood by her, despite inability to provide a cure at this time. I have a

FIGURE 9. Linda: Next Critical Juncture–Desired Contributing Outcome

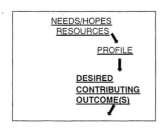

- Restore Linda's sense
of relationship with
God.

FIGURE 10. Linda: Next Critical Juncture–Plan/Integration

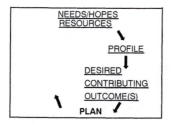

- Medical staff pages chaplain when Linda comes in for treatment.

FIGURE 11. Linda: Next Critical Juncture–Interventions

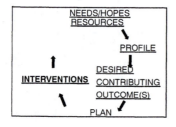

- Validate Linda's anger at God.

- Invite Linda to identify ways God still may be present, active.

sense that this is exactly what Linda's pastor and counselor were doing in their own ways, too.

Linda's own responses, over time, helped her caregivers measure the effects of their interventions (Figure 12). You recall that the hoped-for desired contributing outcome for Linda was restoring in her a sense that God was with her and for her. I want to say right here that we can't know for sure how much of this outcome resulted from our interventions and how much Linda would have come up with on her own. Only God knows that.

Linda's report, and her husband's report, was that her pastoral conversations were a tremendous help to Linda in coping. Linda taught me a lot about trusting God's presence through a continuum of *hope*, from the *immediate* ("let this treatment not make me feel worse") to

FIGURE 12. Linda: Next Critical Juncture–Measurement

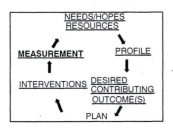

• "I'm still angry, but I'm able to trust God will be with me whatever."

the *intermediate* ("let me survive long enough to see my second grandchild born") to her *ultimate hope* ("God is with me now and I'll be with God when I die.").

Linda died two years after her cancer diagnosis, coping better than many thought she would.

REFERENCE

Andrew Lester. 1995. *Hope in Pastoral Care and Counseling.* Louisville, Ky: Westminister John Knox Press.

A Case Study of Jerry:
Emphasizing Team Communication
Through Use of *The Discipline*

Robert J. Rodrigues Yim, MA, MDiv, BCC

SUMMARY. After the chaplain is well acquainted with *The Discipline* and has begun to implement it in daily pastoral practice, half of the work is done. The further work concerns how and what to communicate to the care team regarding the chaplain's observations. This article begins by offering a pastoral reflection on the chaplain's identity and pastoral practice within a multi-disciplinary care team. The pastoral reflection highlights key theological assertions used by *The Discipline*. The author then identifies the particular problems facing care teams and their communication that the chaplain can anticipate when using *The Discipline*. Thirdly, the author suggests workable, theologically based tools for the resolution of these problems. Lastly, through the case study of "Jerry," the author illustrates both the "how" and "what" components of care team communication using the working elements of *The Discipline*. The "how" component describes the informal and formal relational processes that have contributed to a working partnership. The case study also illustrates the "what" part of care team communication–the structure and delivery of observable and discernible content to physicians and nurses. These materials can ease the transition towards effective pastoral presence on the interdisciplinary care team regarding patient and family/support partner care.

Rev. Robert J. Rodrigues Yim is Anchor Chaplain in Heart Sciences, The Department of Spiritual Care Services, Barnes-Jewish Hospital at Washington University Medical Center, One Barnes-Jewish Hospital Plaza, St. Louis, MO 63110 (E-mail: RJY4551@bjc.org).

KEYWORDS. Chaplain, pastoral care, measurement outcomes, inter-disciplinary team, partnership, communication

THE DISCIPLINE'S APPROACH TO PASTORAL REFLECTION ON CHAPLAIN'S PRACTICE

People do not enter hospitals, hospices or other institutional care settings anonymously. Suffering and pain are frequently familiar companions in such journeys and they diminish the persons' hope and meaning. Secondly, persons are neither defined by their disease nor by a malfunctioning, physical system of their body. As chaplains, each of us not only believes these two assertions, but also recognizes that they touch upon transcendence as experienced in human lives. The rigor of our clinical pastoral education and board certification process as professional chaplains, and the vigor of our everyday pastoral practice compel us to "behold" patients and clients in their personhood and dignity. The theological word, "behold," implies discernible evidence for the mystery; people are more than can be seen, touched, or heard. Chaplains work within the borderlands where the invisible and the visible meet, where the intangible and the tangible are conjoined in reality.

> In the border country one discovers connections, roots, limits, meaning. To live there for a while is like having veils pulled away. In the long run, we find that the border country is, in fact, the place we have always lived, but it is seen in a new and clearer light. (Countryman, 1999)

The art and practice of pastoral care uses a sensitivity and spirituality that "senses" and "explores" what constitutes this "more" for each human life (Carson, 1997). Entering into the qualitative domain of life, the chaplain seeks to understand what the person was like before coming into the healthcare setting. Whereas in the past, chaplains may have looked to denominational affiliation and church attendance as markers for religious involvement, chaplains today are challenged to assess the functionality of spirituality in light of "empirical categories as attuned to human experience" (Pruyser, 1976, p. 62) such as sense of the holy, hope, community, and meaning. In the last century, Pruyser prepared the pastoral ground for this kind of work, asserting the importance of "feelings connected with the experience of the Holy, (rather than) correct thoughts about it" (Pruyser, 1976). Although such an exploration could be adrift in manifold varieties of human characteristics, the chaplain's focused and intentional inquiry attempts to examine how persons functioned in their familiar, native surroundings. These concerns necessarily touch upon quality of life issues–such as mobility, independence, and functionality–that provide a baseline understanding of the patient's experience before the onset of illness.

Most healthcare professionals are likewise interested in baselines. They ask, "What was this person like before coming for help?" and the chaplain is equipped to assess the spiritual domain, "What gave hope, meaning, and a sense of purpose?" While these pastoral skills may be of interest to other care team members, the problem is twofold:

- other care team professionals may be ignorant of the scope of professional chaplains' competencies, and
- the chaplain may not know how to communicate this knowledge succinctly and clearly to the care team in language that they can understand.

The chaplain must be prepared to converse with a wide variety of professionals in a multi-disciplinary dialogue concerning how the care team can best prepare a patient to re-enter life meaningfully and re-shape their routine purposefully. The chaplain's contribution to the care team is a keen understanding and appreciation of the patient's subjective contexts that enrich that person's life beyond religiosity. Through use of the pastoral interview, the chaplain learns what makes up the patient's needs, hopes and resources, and how these are operative in a person's expressed spirituality. People tell chaplains aspects of their lives not shared with others, but they also tell chaplains how they want to share their lives. Chaplains are often confounded by the first part of this equation in an ethical endeavor to safeguard patient/client confidentiality. But, chaplains must be careful to take the opportunity presented by the second half of the equation–countering isolation by promoting social interaction (Oxman, Freeman, & Manheimer, 1995) in assessing spiritual risk (Fitchett, 1999). The chaplain, therefore, can be in a position to make a unique contribution by representing or advocating for the patient's values and beliefs to the care team. With encouragement and reinforcement from all caregivers, these values and beliefs can increase the patient's motivation to participate in their recovery process and healing. I believe that the spark of healing is encouraged when caregivers are willing and interested enough to acknowledge the deepest concerns of patients, namely the search for meaning and significance (Pargament, 1997). Chaplains may know how people are struggling, what is capturing their attention so as to deplete energy needed for healing or drawing from a wellspring that enhances healing. This second type is healing "from the inside out," a more complete form of healing and recovery beyond cure. I have called this a "thriving recovery" (Yim & VandeCreek, 1996).

Problems Facing Care Teams

The first problem facing care teams is that of becoming a team, and secondly, of functioning as a working, collaborative team. To be part of a team, the chaplain needs to be aware that the informal and formal staff relationship processes are equally important. For the chaplain, staff care involves minimally consulting and debriefing with staff members before and after each patient encounter. Such communication actually educates caregivers with the range and repertoire of chaplain's skills and sensibilities. A significant point in these communications occurs when a nurse, physician or ancillary care provider reveals how he or she is personally affected by caring for their patients. To an onlooker, this may appear as two or more professionals talking to each other about professional concerns. A closer view reveals, however, that these caregivers are discussing their humanity and struggles. They are allowing themselves to be vulnerable and personally present for each other rather than competitors. The surprising and wonderful discovery is that neither ought to be exclusive of the other. Becoming a team is built on reliability, dependability, and a solid sense that patients are in good, trustworthy hands. Concretely, this means that chaplains are responsible for educating staff about how best to use them, when to refer, the manner and timeliness of the chaplain's response, and the measure of how people (staff as well as patients) respond to the chaplain's presence. My work with nursing education has taught me that team members are more willing to make referrals to chaplains when chaplains are clear that they neither evangelize nor seek to save lost souls. Meeting people where they are, without imposition of the chaplain's own salvation agenda, is a hallmark of professional CPE training, a fundamental value in the board certification process of chaplains, and a principle of professional eth-ics. Not everyone on the care team may know this.

Becoming a working team takes time and constancy of presence even as it takes time and constancy of presence to deal with people's ultimate questions that arise from illness. How the chaplain uses time and provides pastoral services build the formal processes of profes-sional relationships. Physicians are interested in how their patients are doing, including their emotional and spiritual well-being and they are dependent upon reports from other professionals to inform, guide, and even shape proposed treatments. In the sharing of spiritual assess-ments, pastoral plans, spiritual outcomes and interventions with team members, the chaplain demonstrates what they do and how they con-tribute.

In a working, interdisciplinary team, physicians desire and invite pertinent conversation and competent observation from a variety of consultants, including the professionally-trained chaplain who can guide and inform them as how best to relate to specific patients in their significant contexts. The chaplain can identify the impact of the partic-ular disease process upon the person in terms of coping and conse-quent adjustments as well as the presence or absence of spiritual resources to support healing. Chaplains are trained to assess for these significant elements of patients' lives and can play a considerable role regarding how they hear the team's plan, make informed consent decisions, and participate in their recovery process. In this model, chaplains recommend effective ways in which physicians and nurses can better relate to their patients' concerns, anxieties and struggles, identifying them as significant flags and indicating challenges to their coping and adjustments. Care team decisions can be refined when participants know about the key elements of a patient's spirituality.

Problems in Care Team Communication

Chaplains typically encounter two principal problems in care team communication. The first involves how to translate what is happening with the patient and family into language that physicians, nurses and care team members can clearly understand. The second problem in-volves the chaplain's ability to explicitly share theological reflections on her or his clinical experience with human suffering.

In using *The Discipline,* the chaplain's work is concerned with what is precious or what matters to the patient. In this way, the chaplain considers what people bring into the hospital besides the disease for which they are seeking treatment. The answer is obvious: people bring themselves, and the other parts of their lives including their contexts and relationships that reflect their life's purpose and meaning. Therefore, the chaplain must be equipped to use the language of relationships and lifestyle to better understand

- how people want the world to go;
- how people find themselves in the world; and
- how they are/are not interacting with their environment.

These inquiries aim at the heart of how people pragmatically use their spirituality everyday. The language of relationships and lifestyle is often a strange language to physicians in the clinical setting, but one that they expect chaplains to use in order to convey respect. This basic respect is not only for patients and their support partners, but also for physicians and care team members. Concretely, this means that professional chaplains do the hard work of creating a profile, desired contributing outcomes, plan, interventions and evaluation for each patient visited. The usual tendency at this point is for chaplains to share their entire activity with the patient, or to relate their experience of what it is like to be with the patient/family, or to confound team communication with theological jargon that cuts off further discussion from the team.

Chaplain's Tools for Resolution

Charles Gerkin (1984) was the first to coin the term "clinical theology" as the appearance of patient's theological questions in concrete experience. In *The Living Human Document,* he advocates " . . . a more even-handed interdisciplinary approach to reflection on that [pastoral] practice which does not subordinate theology to psychotherapeutic theory or subsume psychotherapeutic language into a heavy-handed insistence on the authority of theological word usage and God talk" (p. 33). He envisions a clinical theological language that includes, not excludes, the interdisciplinary team. Just as physicians can use codified, technical medical terms which lay persons do not readily understand, chaplains may unwittingly use theological jargon, God talk or church-speak that are not part of usual physician vocabulary. For example, a chaplain may faithfully report that Mrs. Jones is afraid that "she will die and not go to heaven." The physician would be justified in having a stunned look on his face, wondering why the chaplain is telling her or him all this, as the physician has no control over whether a person enters the pearly gates. But if the chaplain communicates that Mrs. Jones is experiencing "anxiety over fate and mortality" (Patterson, 1985), the physician would certainly know much about morbidity and mortality and would certainly desire a fate other than death for the patient. The difference in language reveals the chaplain's acute awareness as to who is receiving the communication as well as a clear intention that the chaplain wishes to be sufficiently heard and understood so as to invite further inquiry and exploration from the care team. *The Discipline* uses clinical theology that dynamically captures a person's spirituality for healing and makes that knowledge known to the care team for the best care of the patient and family/support partners.

The issue of clinical theological language will become even more paramount as the understanding of holism evolves from the work of scientists and thinkers such as Antonio Demasio (1994), Candace B. Pert (1999), as well as George Lakoff and Mark Johnson (1999). The whole understanding of human beings is being re-defined from the conventional view of Descartes' mechanistic *Cogito, ergo sum* ("I think, therefore I am") that supports the superiority of reason towards a more comprehensive appreciation of how such a dualism does not stand up against the recent scientific evidence regarding the chemical-molecular basis of emotions, memory and neural processes alongside cognitive functioning. Damasio (1994) highlights "the ability to plan one's future as a social being as something uniquely human" (p. 19). As the mind-body connection opens up more and more to include the realm of emotions, chaplains will be faced with another challenge of how to intellectually address such issues from a theological perspective and remain in conversation with these disciplines. Failure to do so would further contribute to the current problems facing professional chaplaincy as an "absent profession" (Vandecreek, 1999), whereby professional authors do not acknowledge the chaplain's expertise in spiritual and religious care.

Case Study: The Story of Jerry

Every serious illness involves an anxiety-producing encounter with non-being: "Different kinds of illnesses, however, may give rise to somewhat different configurations of anxiety" (Patterson, 1985, p. 249). Though 'Jerry' is a fictional name to protect patient confidentiality, this case study is based upon a real pastoral encounter.

Communicating Needs, Hopes and Resources.

Jerry was scared, needing reassurance regarding open-heart valve replacement surgery for the most severe case of cardiomyopathy seen by the cardiac team. His enlarged heart was diminishing his active lifestyle, causing fatigue and shortness of breath. He was unable to sustain activities that affected his own ability to care for himself and affected his supportive role of his wife. My first pastoral visit with Jerry and his spouse took place while he was awaiting cardiac catherization in the pre-procedure holding area. The cardiac catherization would render a definitive picture of the blood flow through the heart and determine the extent of heart valve damage. Jerry was lying flat on his back with his wife sitting in a chair besides him. His wife was also scared, feeling helpless and yet trying to smile so as to bolster her husband's disposition.

By appearance, Jerry was a muscular man in early retirement with his physically fit wife. Both had won Senior Olympic gold medals in weight-lifting competitions for their respective age divisions. This was a serious hobby and mutual interest that both enjoyed and shared together. Competitive weightlifting was their common activity around which they organized their travel in early retirement, constructing new identities and meanings for their shared lives. Weightlifting was also a family activity enjoyed by their one adult son. In the pastoral interview, I asked what would be his hopes for his life should surgery be in his future, and he revealed that he hoped to win the Senior Olympics gold medal in the free throw competition! Though Jerry was affiliated with a religious denomination, his relentless spirit seemed to draw more resourcefulness from meditation practices that he and his wife previously used for relaxation. In his hectic life as well as in his anxiety over his fate and mortality, Jerry had "forgotten" the value of meditation for his present state of mind. Since the chaplain needs to succinctly communicate Needs, Hopes and Resources to the interdisciplinary team, I usually give myself the following challenge: How could I encapsulate them in a minute's worth of words and calmly deliver the message?

Communicating Profile

Jerry's unfolding narrative disclosed an individual who mechanistically pushed his body into a danger zone, thereby threatening his health for purposes of achievement and recognition. He did not yet know his threshold that would indicate when he had gone too far and was doing damage to his body. As these impressions built within myself, I used *The Discipline* to temper my impulse to correct behavior. Instead, *The Discipline* kept my professionalism on track by having me seek an understanding of Jerry's Sense of the Holy, Meaning, Community and Personal Purpose. Through the pastoral dialogue, Jerry told me that he did not "want to be cheated of his future" (sense of holy), wanted a "lifestyle of fitness and health (meaning), felt supported when surrounded by his wife and son (community), and that he desired a "life without fear" (purpose). Not only did these expressed values represent how Jerry did theology for his own life experiences, I am comfortable in using his quotes in an APIE format (Assessment, Plan, Intervention, Evaluation) when entering the chaplain's notes into the medical record. The use of the patient's own words imparted how the patient understood himself within an acceptable structure of a charting format.

Communicating Desired Contributing Outcomes

In working with outcomes, chaplains need to understand that the outcomes are made from the profile/spiritual assessment, and are formed before the chaplain puts together the pastoral plan. Outcomes are not "what is left at the end" of the pastoral encounter nor are they the residue following success or failure of the chaplain's interventions. Instead, the chaplain puts together specific, concrete, behavior-based outcomes that describe what the patient wants for herself or himself. In this case, I specified two outcomes: (a) " ... *so that* Jerry may better identify his threshold of stress and when he is in the danger zone of having pushed himself too hard"; and (b) " ... *so that* Jerry can help himself relax before surgery and allow the doctors to do their work." Notice that the language of outcomes is often prefaced with terms like "so that ... " or "in order that ... " As the chaplain forms well-defined outcomes, the chaplain may use what patients want for their own personhood or future. Such an approach keeps outcomes within the grasp and manageability of the patient's desires and away from the temptation that the chaplain's job is to push patients towards chaplain's goals. Another significant consideration in forming well-defined outcomes is to remember that chaplain's outcomes must be mindful of the overall team's outcomes for the patient. This mindfulness maintains a vital connection between chaplain and care team, thereby requiring the chaplain to talk regularly with the interdisciplinary team regarding what is the team's plan for the patient.

Communicating Plan

Doing the work of forming well-defined outcomes will assist the chaplain in specifying a pastoral plan. The pastoral plan may outline the specific steps that the chaplain envisions for the patient's progress. In Jerry's case, my plan had three steps: (1) Demonstrate and teach Jerry a guided imagery that he can practice before procedure/surgery; (2) Have Jerry experience his body relaxing in order to bolster his confidence and pre-surgery disposition; and (3) Explain when the tube down the throat will be removed. I chose these three steps for my plan because, as I listened to his story, I was able to identify clearly his anxieties as he tried to imagine the course of treatment ahead of him. Jerry's anxieties centered on fears that he might survive surgery but would be incapacitated by stroke. The waiting was tortuous for him. His last fear was about intubation and not being able to swallow–swallowing being an unconscious habit that occurred whenever he was stressed. All this built into spiritual distress. The goal of the pastoral plan was to reduce stress in the patient-defined areas so that the patient may begin to cope and adjust to the realities of his physical condition and environment. For the team to know that one of its members, i.e., the chaplain, was actively working with these patient areas of concern encourages them to excel in their jobs.

Communicating Interventions

The team needs to know whether the chaplain achieved the plan. Ethically, if a caregiver spots a problem, then that caregiver is responsible for doing something about it. Listing the chaplain's interventions informs the team of what approaches were used for a particular patient and what else the chaplain intends to contribute towards the patient's welfare and healing. In Jerry's case, I listed four interventions: (1) Achieved plan. (2) Goal was to favorably dispose Jerry for cardiac cath and open heart surgery. (3) Will continue to support spouse/family while Jerry is in O.R. (4) Will monitor Jerry and provide spiritual support as needed and appropriate.

Communicating Evaluation/Measurement

It is important for chaplains to evaluate or measure the effectiveness of their interventions. Too often, the chaplain misunderstands evaluation to mean that the patient liked the chaplain and wants the chaplain to return. Certainly, the pleasant temperament of the chaplain is valuable. However, evaluation looks for measurable evidence of change in the patient's behavior that indicates improved coping and adjustment. In Jerry's case, I listed in the chart two measurements: (1) Jerry achieved internal locus of control so that he was able to reduce anxiety over his fate and mortality; and (2) Jerry was able to manage his fear of surgery such that his attitude towards the future was strengthened and realistic.

CONCLUSION

The use of *The Discipline* is certainly hard work, but it becomes easier with consistent practice. The largest incentive is that the professional chaplain creates "best practices" that create invaluable good!

REFERENCES

Carson, Timothy L. (1997). *Liminal Reality and Transformational Power.* (New York: University Press of America).

Countryman, L. Wm. (1999). *Living on the Border of the Holy: Renewing the Priesthood of All.* (Harrisburg: Morehouse Publishing), p. 8.

Damasio, Antonio R. (1994). *Descartes' Error: Emotion, Reason and the Human Brain* (New York: Avon Books).

Fitchett, George. (1999). Screening for Spiritual Risk. *Chaplaincy Today* 15 (1), 2-12.

Gerkin, Charles V. (1984). *The Living Human Document: Re-Visioning Pastoral Counseling in a Hermeneutical Mode.* (Nashville: Abingdon Press), p. 33.

Lakoff, George & Johnson, M. (1999). *Philosophy in the Flesh: The Embodied Mind and Its Challenges to Western Thought* (New York: Basic Books).

Oxman, T.E., Freeman, D.E. Jr., & Manheimer, E.D. (1995). Lack of Social Participation or Religious Strength and Comfort as Risk Factors for Death After Cardiac Surgery in the Elderly. *Psychosomatic Medicine* 57, 5-15.

Pargament, K.L. (1997). *The Psychology of Religion and Coping: Theory, Research, Practice.* (New York: The Guilford Press), p. 90.

Patterson, George W. (1985). Pastoral Care of the Coronary Patient and Family. *The Journal of Pastoral Care* 39 (3), 249-261. (In this important article, Patterson uses Paul Tillich's classic analysis of persons' awareness of non-being as experienced as anxiety and existing in three fundamental forms: the anxiety over fate and mortality, over guilt and regret, and over meaninglessness and helplessness. Patterson adds a fourth: the anxiety over separation and isolation.)

Pert, Candace B. (1999). *Molecules of Emotion* (New York: Simon and Schuster, Inc).

Pruyser, Paul W. (1976). *The Minister As Diagnostician: Personal Problems in Pastoral Perspective* (Philadelphia: The Westminister Press), p. 62.

VandeCreek, Larry. (1999). Professional Chaplaincy: An Absent Profession? *The Journal of Pastoral Care* 53(4), p. 417-432.

Yim, R. & Vandecreek, L. (1996). Unbinding Grief and Life Losses for Thriving Recovery After Open Heart Surgery: How Pastoral Care Works in a Managed Care Setting. *The Caregiver Journal* 12(2), 8-11.

A Case Study Using *The Discipline* with a Clinical Team

Janet R. Crane, MTS, BCC

SUMMARY. Health care delivery in hospitals and clinics promotes an interdisciplinary team approach. This article presents the use of *The Discipline* though the involvements of the chaplain as part of the Infectious Disease team as together they addressed the inherent spirituality of one HIV/AIDS patient. This narrative recounts the unfolding events of the patient's life and describes the use of *The Discipline* during a very difficult time period for the patient and the staff. The experience can serve as a model for other health care teams who must manage difficult, deteriorating patients.

Janet R. Crane was Staff Chaplain with Spiritual Care Services, Barnes-Jewish Hospital at Washington University, One Barnes-Jewish Hospital Plaza, St. Louis, MO 63110.

The author wishes to recognize the clinical team from the Infectious Disease Department of Internal Medicine who worked closely with Ces and assisted in preparing this case study: William Powderly, MD, J. Russell Little, MD, Pablo Tebas, MD, Victoria Fraser, MD, Linda Mundy, MD, Amy Hunter, RN. To be commended for their participation are the Fellows, Hillary Babcock, MD, Kristin Mondy, MD, and Richard Starlin, MD; social worker, Lynn Green, MSW; case manager, Deborah Mentz, RN; the nurses and patient techs on Unit 11200, who rotated in Ces' care. The author also thanks the members of staff at Barnes-Jewish Hospital and at Helena Hatch Special Care Center at Washington University, St. Louis, MO, especially Debbi Gase, RN, Amy Hunter, RN, and Kate Rogers, RN.

KEYWORDS. Chaplain, pastoral care, measurement, outcomes, interdisciplinary team

BACKGROUND

The team approach has developed into a normative means of providing effective care for patients and has received much attention. The purpose here is not to address the need for health care teams or to argue about which professionals are essential or ancillary to the team. Rather, the purpose is to offer some experiences that exhibit how *The Discipline* was effective within best care practices, including ways in which it was integrated and accountable for patient care and functioned within the dynamics of the team.

How does one begin to understand the use of *The Discipline* within the team? In a study by a University of Minnesota Health Sciences Task Force on Interdisciplinary Health Team Development (Gardebring et al., 1996), patients perceived a need for integrated health care teams because of (1) poor communication, (2) duplication of services, and (3) lack of patient focus. (It is noted that the Task Force did not include a chaplain or clergy representative and only addressed Medicine, Nursing, Pharmacy and Public Health.) These three factors parallel the need for better integration of health care teams in general and speak of our experience. Generally, members of the Infectious Disease team had worked at one time or another with a chaplain. Yet, these three limitations were also found within our team and concerned communication, misunderstanding of the expertise of chaplains and spiritual care services, and the patient in our care.

Primary care physicians traditionally directed the health care interventions and assigned the responsibility for those interventions. Today, patient care is coordinated by many different professionals who have a language and practice of their own. In another effort to collaborate, we have concurred as members of the ID team on this paper. We present here a focus on *The Discipline* as an example of the interaction and contribution that routinely takes place within this multidisciplinary team. Other special team projects include research to be published on the subject of the role of prayer and women's decision-making to take HIV medication.

The chaplain was the resource for educating the team on the role of the chaplain, for developing integration and accountability with the team for intentional evaluation and improvement of pastoral care, effective and direct communication about the spirituality of patients and families, and for recognizing patterns in the healing of patients which involved unique spiritual dynamics. Members of the team had varying experience with chaplains and the use of spiritual care services.

The author has participated in *The Discipline* since 1992. Chaplains were part of the ID team on a limited basis until January 1998. At this time, a grant from the institution provided a full time chaplain for the hospital patients with HIV and for their continuity of care upon discharge both through the Helena Hatch Special Care Center (HHSCC) for women, the ID clinic, and/or to home. This was an important opportunity to make a consistent pastoral care contribution to patient care. In a study, the presence of a chaplain and the availability of spiritual care services in a clinic as well as a hospital setting were shown to be effective places to address spiritual needs of patients (Mandziuk, 1996).

USING THE DISCIPLINE

To understand the use of *The Discipline* and the unique contribution chaplains can make, we present the case study of a patient during her recent hospitalization, referring to her by the pseudonym, Ces. Ces' care involved the best and often frustrating efforts of the ID team. To maintain confidentiality, only essential information has been given.

THE MATTER OF CES

The following are notes taken and summarized from the medical chart:

> Ces is a 32 year old, African American female, divorced mother of two children, a daughter aged 11 and a son aged 14. Ces is well known to the Infectious Disease Service since 5-16-95. She is HIV-positive since May, 1995, non-compliant with highly active antiretroviral therapy (HAART), infected with genital herpes, has end stage renal disease secondary to hypertension, who was started on hemodialysis since 10-98. Her recent CD4

count as of 5-3-99 was 206 (23.1%) and her viral load was 94,138. On 9-14-99, Ces was admitted through the ER with abdominal pain. She was discharged on 9-22-99 to home; however, she was to have a colonoscopy on 9-22-99, but refused to drink the prep and this could not be done. On 10-4-99, she was admitted to the psychiatry service for depression. She was returned to the medicine service to resume hemodialysis. When she was medically stable, she stated she did not wish to return to psychiatry service and she was discharged home. She was admitted to the hospital on 10-15-99 with evidence of a subdural hematoma and seizure. It is unclear which came first. Her subdural hematoma resolved, but she continued to exhibit bizarre combative behavior, which is attributed to HIV encephalopathy. Ces was admitted from an outside hospital to the medical ICU already intubated. She was restrained because she attempted to pull her line during hemodialysis. Other complications of note included persistent fever of unknown origin, which was later determined to be due to gluteal abscesses, which were drained. She was restarted on antiretroviral medications on 11-16-99. She remained afebrile and had a dramatic improvement in her mental status. She was discharged to a nursing home on 12-10-99 for physical therapy, rehabilitation, and observation for her medications.

THE QUESTIONS FOR CARE:
NEEDS, HOPES, RESOURCES

One look at Ces intubated, restrained, and receiving hemodialysis in the medical ICU shortly after admission revealed her multiple and profound needs. The dilemma with Ces for her 10-15-99 admission to the hospital for the team of physicians, pharmacist, nurses and chaplain was:

- What should be done for Ces?
- What would Ces want us to do for her? What would be a satisfactory outcome to Ces or her family?
- Who knows what Ces would want based on conversations and consistent behavior patterns? Who can relate to Ces and whom will Ces relate to?

• How can a care plan and goals be set that assist in moving Ces toward the next step of the healing process? Who will participate in this?

These questions for her care came from the previous experiences of members of the team with Ces. Corporately, it was difficult to acknowledge or discuss what Ces' hopes and resources were with any certainty. Asking the questions recognized that she had hopes and resources. In conversations with physicians, nurses, social workers and chaplains during other hospitalizations and in the HHSCC clinic, Ces said she would like "for this disease to be over," "to be left alone," and "not to have to think about HIV because it made her depressed." She also talked about her children, particularly her son, her many boyfriends and their failed relationships, and her mother and sister who were the only ones who knew about her HIV. She liked "looking good" and "having a job and her own money." Her present condition by our assessment was her worst nightmare.

While her needs were many, the team assumed her hopes and resources were limited and minimal. A resource, identifiable to the team, which had been operative in the past, was her recognition of the chaplain by smiling and making eye contact with her. When extubated, Ces could call her by name even when she did not know where she was nor recognize her family members. This was attributed to the frequent contact Ces had with the chaplain at HHSCC and the hospital. Another resource was her appreciation, by thanking them, for the attention given by the patient techs when they fixed her hair. These were notable to the team. The skill was the ability to take her day-to-day presentation of her needs and organize it to include her faintest hopes as we knew and understood them and the resources as we continued to discover them.

A PATIENT PROFILE OF CES?

Discussions concerning Ces' medical care often focused on nursing, social work and financial concerns. The physicians that rotated in the ID service had previous experience with her in the hospital and/or in the clinic. She had a reputation with physicians of non-compliance regarding medication and treatment. She explained her missed hemodialysis appointments and poor pill taking with "I didn't want to" or

"It makes me feel bad." She would describe herself as depressed, but was not willing to address the issue. She would complain that people were in her business if encouraged to be compliant. Nurses and social workers in the clinic followed up with her concerning her HIV and her needs. The chaplain, who followed HIV patients both in the hospital and the clinic, interacted with Ces occasionally by phone. Ces and the chaplain established a significant rapport and relationship for Ces to confide in the chaplain about issues of relationships, hope and her understanding of God and her illness. Her mother and sister, who knew of Ces' medical conditions, participated in the care of Ces' children and visited her in the hospital. Both the mother and the sister had spoken to the chaplain on several other occasions about their concern for Ces.

She was passive in her interaction with the physicians and nurses until her last two hospitalizations. Upon her last hospitalization, she exhibited aggressive behavior, which included shouting at staff when giving her medications, refusing the preparation for tests and rejecting the presence of her family. The chaplain who related to her over several years was asked to cut her visits short by Ces. She said to the chaplain whose visits she had requested and expected previously that her presence was only a reminder of her HIV disease. Ces' behavior had significantly changed. The hospital social worker and case manager consulted with the ID team and family about appropriate discharge planning. Ces, being an HIV patient with multiple medical problems, was recognized as a financial concern to the hospital.

Ces had repeated to almost every caregiver that she did not want to live with HIV. She wanted it "all to be over." She wanted to be left "alone" and not encouraged to take medication or get medical treatment. Her idea of God was that he had control of everything and she just had to accept what God sent. Studies have explored the meaning of spirituality and spiritual beliefs among people living with HIV and women, in particular, and how they are beneficial or a hindrance (Kaldjian et al., 1998) (Guillory et al., 1997).

The components of Ces' spiritual profile functioned primarily like stumbling blocks for her medical care. For this hospitalization, it could have been assumed that Ces would have wanted us to discontinue treatment, i.e., hemodialysis, and let her die. What difference and how does her life script, relationships, faith commitments, world view, role as mother, daughter, sister, Baptist religious history, sense of beauty and/or will make for Ces right now in her present context? Was her fighting an effort to stay alive or a resistance to treatment in order to die? The function of these, we hoped to engage for her healing and well-being.

DESIRED CONTRIBUTING OUTCOMES?

When Ces was extubated and transferred to a medical firm, her mental status exhibited signs of hallucinations and paranoia due to her HIV encephalopathy. Her hemodialysis was continued. However, several incidents in the hemodialysis unit that included Ces verbally abusing the staff, removing the access line, and spraying blood in the unit, put the continuation of hemodialysis in jeopardy due to the risk to staff and other patients. She was heavily sedated to make the hemodialysis possible. In her room, she was restrained and attended by a series of sitters. Her chief complaint was that people, chiefly the staff, were out to kill her.

The team's desired outcomes were for the patient to become sufficiently calm, to keep her comfortable and to make medical care possible. Sensible conversation was not yet possible with Ces, so we had to move forward in her best interest. The desired contributing outcomes from the pastoral care perspective carried the team outcomes into the effects we hoped intentional actions on our part would attain for Ces. Drawing on past experience, HIV patients generally show a limited capacity to trust. Ces expressed her mistrust of family, friends and clinical staff by anger toward people who cared about her. She interpreted them to be "in her business" or "causing her trouble." In her present mental condition, it was translated into who "knows about me" and who "is trying to kill me." The desired contributing outcomes were twofold: for the patient to establish trust with at least one person who would partner with her and to reduce her anxiety. Both were necessary for her comfort and care. These outcomes were observable and measurable and could be communicated to the team on a routine basis. The outcomes could also be referred to with Ces.

Throughout Ces' fifty-seven day hospital stay, the desired contributing outcomes varied in the intensity of their desire by the team. The mental status of Ces and the medical assessments and recommendations for her care changed frequently.

THE PLAN?

The plan for her spiritual care given the complication of her medical diagnoses and treatment was quite simple. Because Ces responded to the chaplain, the chaplain was designated as a resource for establishing trusting relationships with other caregivers. Because Ces recognized the chaplain during every visit, could refer to her by name, and engage in conversation, the plan was for the chaplain to visit Ces every day. It was hoped with the myriad staff attending Ces that she would have at least one person spend time with her that she related with. Frequently, during rounds, she initiated the conversation with Ces. The staff contacted the chaplain when Ces would become acutely combative or when she refused to take her medication. But establishing a trusting relationship with Ces and reducing her anxiety was not the responsibility of the chaplain alone. The physicians who rotated in the service each in their turn responded to Ces with compassion and concern. Nurses and patient techs also tried to involve Ces in a trusting relationship by speaking to her reassuringly and commending her when she cooperated. Ces continued to have only infrequent lucid moments presumed to be the result of HIV encephalopathy and sedation, leaving the team with little indication if or how Ces participated in the plan. Indicators of trust or lessened anxiety were her engagement of conversation with staff and her willingness to follow directives for her care, such as pill taking and hygiene.

INTERVENTIONS

The plan was in place, but the interventions both medical and spiritual were frustrating for the staff because they did not seem to succeed. She constantly refused to take her medication. The plan called for the nurses to call the chaplain she always recognized and the chaplain would ask Ces to take her medication. Usually, she would take her pills immediately. If she did not, the chaplain would engage her in a few minutes of conversation and Ces would take the pills.

Ces needed to remain restrained to prevent her from pulling her lines or harming herself or staff. Midway in her hospitalization, she was confined to a netted bed in an effort to give her some freedom. However, she pulled one of her lines and had to again have wrist restraints.

Monday through Friday, the chaplain visited Ces for at least fifteen minutes in an effort to connect with Ces, offer her comfort and to pray with her. Ces had asked the chaplain once in her confused state of mind to pray with her. On following visits when Ces would be confused or agitated she would respond calmly to the chaplain's suggestion to pray. The daily visits were brief because Ces' attention was short. The short visits, at times twice a day, seemed to be comforting to her for at least the length of the visit.

After thirty days in the hospital, she was restarted on highly active antiretroviral therapy (HAART) that meant additional medication. Because the pills demanded strict adherence to be effective, Ces could not miss doses. When the team chaplain was not in the hospital, she would speak to Ces over the phone if necessary. Rarely was it necessary for the chaplain to come in to assure Ces sufficiently for her to take her pills.

After six weeks, a meeting with Ces' mother and sister was arranged to consider a plan of care for Ces. Her family experienced Ces' lack of progress. She recognized them occasionally, but seldom remembered their visits or those of her children. They observed her agitation and mental status. They were aware and understood Ces' medical diagnoses related to her HIV and renal failure. Ces had expressed to them her feelings about living with HIV, having to undergo hemodialysis, relating to medical staff and taking medication. Her family identified her inability to trust other people including her family and friends. They worried about her on the religious level because she found it difficult to participate in their church community. She had complained that the people in the congregation were judging her. They repeated what she had said to the chaplain that "God was the only one in control." The intense conversation concluded that treatment would continue at its present level for another week. While the family thought that Ces would probably not want further aggressive treatment, they were willing to continue if it seemed to be in her best interest by the physicians. Another meeting would be arranged to evaluate Ces' progress.

MEASUREMENT

The plan was followed. With the passage of time and little change of Ces' combative behavior, frustration and weariness made hopefulness for Ces' recovery diminish. Reflection on the desired outcomes yielded Ces' ability to establish trust to promote her recovery and to cope with her anxiety. These were not limited to Ces' pill taking, reduction of outbursts in hemodialysis, interaction with physicians and nurses and animated conversations with the chaplain of the team. She still had hallucinations of dogs and rats in her room and bed. She was not always oriented to the hospital.

About five days from the family meeting, the Infectious Disease team noted that Ces became more sensible in her conversation. Change on several levels became remarkable. Nurses noticed that when she called out, she would politely add "please" and "thanks." A former boyfriend came to visit Ces and she interacted with him in a friendly, appropriate manner. In her conversations with the chaplain, she confided that he did not know about her HIV. She did not remember what happened to her. She wanted the chaplain to talk to her mother about where she would go when she was discharged. Especially important to her was that she was feeling more like herself again. Ces asked for her favorite candy and foods. Nurses experimented with periods when she was unrestrained in the presence of the chaplain. Within a day, she was able to remain unrestrained. However, it was not clear medically what was contributing to the change although it was presumed that the HIV medications were taking effect.

Another family meeting was arranged. How to involve Ces was not clear to the team. When Ces was informed that a family meeting was about to convene, she asked the attending physician if there was anything he would say to them that he could not say to her. She wished to be present and she was. She then participated in her own discharge plan, which addressed Ces' needs, hopes and resources. Strategies involved physical therapy before discharge, adherence to HAART, discharge to a nursing home and follow up in the HHSCC clinic. The chaplain facilitated communication between Ces and the social worker looking for nursing home placement, discussed the situation with the other team members and offered support to the family as they coped with Ces' children and new living arrangements. Ces, her family and the team planned for her to be routinely contacted by the chaplain to provide communication concerning her medical care. More important though, follow up by the chaplain would foster a link of trust between Ces and those caring for her.

REFLECTIONS ON THE DISCIPLINE *AND THE ID TEAM*

Pastoral care has been a traditional service within many health care systems. In some settings, physicians and medical staff have counted on chaplains to attend to the spiritual and religious needs of the patients. Chaplains sought to participate with patients in engaging their spirituality to make a difference in their recovery and healing. What we learned from the spiritual perspective as a team with Ces was how the spiritual functioned for Ces and what difference it made for her. It took a team effort to communicate on the many levels of her needs and treatment, to participate as a team by respecting and perceiving the contribution made by team members and others, and to help the patient focus on her best interest even when she could not understand it herself. The ID team, which addressed the spiritual care of Ces and honored the advocacy of the chaplain for her, remained hopeful through her hospitalization and insisted that hemodialysis be continued. On the other hand, the renal team in the dialysis unit considered hemodialysis for Ces as futile.

Anyone of the team could have established a relationship with the patient. The relationship with the chaplain was significant because it operated as a bridge between the patient and the team and a means of providing a continuum of care. *The Discipline* was an effective means within our best care for Ces, for integration and accountability for her and within the dynamics of the team.

Having a discipline for pastoral care giving was useful in identifying the uniqueness and the commonality of Ces with other patients in our care. Noting patterns in spiritual dynamics with other patients helped us focus on the acute care reality of Ces. We grappled every day with the questions of what Ces would want and who could best speak for her. Day-by-day we searched for ways to attend to Ces and promote her well-being. The day when Ces could respond the team recognized that she was again participating in her own care, not out of mistrust, but out of trust.

The limitations of this case study reflect the fact it is focused on the extreme situation of one person with HIV and how the ID team which had a chaplain, responded. Other spiritual care services could be useful without the involvement of a clinical team. We encourage research studies in the field of spiritual care to better understand the discrete contributions compassionate, professional, clinically integrated spiritual care can make and how they occur. Our experience indicates *The Discipline* helped substantiate both the care process for one person and the structure for good research.

The most immediate implication of *The Discipline* within this case study illustrates that it can be an effective tool for integrating pastoral care into a clinical team for the benefit of the patient and continuum of care before, during and after hospitalization. Key factors in its use are communication with the team formally or informally, clarity of the role of the chaplain and the participation of the patient.

REFERENCES

Gardebring, S.S. et al. (1996). Developing health care teams [On-line]. Available: www.ahc.umn.edu/tf/ihtd.html.

Guillory, J. et al. (1997). An exploration of the meaning and use of spirituality among women with HIV/AIDS. *Alternative Therapies,* 3(5), 55-60.

Kilburn, K. (1990). Creating and maintaining as effective interdisciplinary research team. *R & D Management,* 20(2), 131-139.

Mandzuik, P. (1996). Is there a chaplain in your clinic? *Journal of Religion and Health,* 35(1), 5-9.

Palmer, C. et al. (1996). Religious evaluation of lung transplant patients. *Caregiver Journal,* 12(3), 9-19.

Schofield, R. et al. (1999). Interdisciplinary teams in health care and human services settings: Are they effective? *Health and Social Work,* 24 (3), 210-219.

The Discipline:
Its Impact on My Theological Perspective, Pastoral Identity and Practice

Robert J. Rodrigues Yim, MA, MDiv, BCC

SUMMARY. This article is a personal interpretation of how *The Discipline* has re-formulated the pastoral identity, practice, and theology of a board certified chaplain providing ministry to patients in the heart sciences. His reflections take into account his history as an ordained priest and as a professionally trained chaplain. The article reflects his struggles and theological transformations, demonstrating how a theological base may emerge from the interpretative reflection on *The Discipline*. The article describes the uneasy internal and external processes that occurred in and around him during that transformation. His story also attests to growth made "from the inside out" as a chaplain within a generative multi-faith department.

KEYWORDS. Chaplain, theology, pastoral care, measurement, outcome, identity, practice

Rev. Robert J. Rodrigues Yim is Anchor Chaplain in Heart Sciences, The Department of Spiritual Care Services, Barnes-Jewish Hospital at Washington University Medical Center, One Barnes-Jewish Hospital Plaza, St. Louis, MO 63110 (E-mail: RJY4551@bjc.org).

PASTORAL VISIONING BORN OF MATURE, GENERATIVE FAITH COMMUNITIES

In my day-to-day chaplaincy work of visiting heart patients and spiritually supporting them within their relational contexts, I have for nearly ten years consistently used *The Discipline* of Pastoral Care Giving as an effective pastoral methodology. It is a reflective tool that helps me to better understand what is actually transpiring within pastoral encounters. In this article, I use my ten years in health care ministry as a periscope to illustrate how *The Discipline* has significantly contributed to the shaping and transformation of my own pastoral self, identity, theology and function during the last twenty-five years of ministry. This has not been an easy personal journey, but a call that has challenged me to struggle with the same influences that perplex every health care chaplain yet to emerge from these forces intact and in meaningful and purposeful ways.

I joined the Pastoral Care Department at Barnes Hospital in 1990 as a Roman Catholic priest after serving fifteen years in stateside parishes and foreign missions in Latin America. At that juncture of my pastoral life, I was witness to a variety of pastoral visions from diverse sources that cumulatively set the stage for my own theological transformation as a hospital chaplain. The first pastoral vision was that of my own Archbishop at the time, the Most Rev. John May. Based upon his own previous hospital experiences as a young priest, this Archbishop had a far-reaching, inclusive pastoral vision that his priests should not be set apart from, but work alongside with chaplains in the pastoral care department. He wanted his priests who were assigned to hospital ministry to be as professionally qualified as the rest of the chaplaincy staff even if this meant going back to school for more education.

The second pastoral vision came by way of a work interview. On Christmas Eve of 1989 at 3:30 P.M. in the afternoon, after everyone had finished their holiday parties at work, the Vice-President of Human Resources asked me only one question, "Would I visit only Catholic patients?" In hindsight, this was probably a *pro forma* interview with the to-be-expected answer that would quickly end the interview so that he could join his family for the holiday break. With a quizzical look on my face, my unexpected answer to him was, "No! Why should I visit only Catholic patients? Catholics aren't the only ones who get sick!" This Jewish administrator, a bit caught off guard by a response that he did not anticipate, continued the interview for another hour and a half after which he hired me. His question would later seem a portent of future diverse, multi-faith approaches to spiritual care. The powerful lesson presented to me at this point in my pastoral life was that the wider communities in which we all live and work also influence and shape the emergence of pastoral visioning of how to be in the world as a caring presence. Pastoral visioning, as lively interactions between caring and concerned individuals who look at and explore the connections between faith and health, takes place also outside the confines of our denominations and adjudicatories. Through a process of greater inclusivity and partnership, I would learn that to function as a chaplain would be a distinct pastoral genre from the familiar worlds of sacramental and congregational care.

The third pastoral vision came by way of a new department director, the Rev. Arthur M. Lucas, who changed the conventional assignment of clergy chaplains from serving their respective denominations to working within clinical service lines and particular disease processes. This was the start of how my own pastoral identity and approach would shift. Pastoral care would be a larger world than sacramental priesthood, and chaplaincy would involve a wider community of faith perspectives. I entered an ACPE CPE residency with the St. Louis Cluster in 1990-1991 and simultaneously started a Master's Program at St. Louis University in Pastoral Health Care. This was a one-of-a-kind interdisciplinary pastoral care degree from the School of Public Health put together by the pastoral vision of a forward-looking Daughter of Charity, Sr. Marie Agnew, Ph.D. In this fourth pastoral vision working within the paradigm of community-based healthcare, Sr. Agnew's educational program further presented a vision of how chaplains could interact and converse as interdisciplinary partners with physicians and nurses around patients' care that would include patients' spirituality and sensibilities. What a wonderful mix of unintentional, yet complementary pastoral visions generated from a mix of seemingly unrelated sources–a Roman Catholic Archbishop, a Jewish clinically-trained psychologist working in healthcare, a Methodist Elder, and a Roman Catholic woman religious educator–all of which led me to and pointed a path for learning a fully integrated ministry to the sick and dying. Each of these community leaders represented mature faith communities that themselves were generative of faith, sources of religious insight and ministry, as well as better able to witness to the society in which they lived and were a member (Whitehead & Whitehead).

By 1991, I had completed my residency program, and from 1991-1993, I was among several, new clinical-line staff chaplains in the department. In our spiritual dialogue and joint reflections, we became contributing participants in the creation of *The Discipline*. Multiple mergers made these tumultuous times for the hospital. External as well as internal demands demanded our energies and attention as we sought to further develop our professionalism as chaplains. By 1993, when I had completed my Master's Program at St. Louis University and an M.Div. degree at Kenrick Seminary in preparation for my application to the then College of Chaplains, our institutional and departmental identities had become multi-disciplinary and multi-faith through the creation of Barnes-Jewish Hospital and Spiritual Care Services Department.

What grounded me through all these mergers and transitions was an emerging, experientially based pastoral vision that found concrete expression in the *The Discipline*. It was constructed by the community or chaplains and denominationally respectful of where persons were in their understanding of their spiritual and religious well-being. While I was well acquainted with the Roman Catholic perspective, this time would stretch me to encompass and learn about other faith traditions. It brought a sense of the Holy, of Hope, Community and Meaning to others' lives. *The Discipline* helped me to be more faithful in opening my pastoral life to others as well as teaching me how to invite others to open their spiritual lives for healing. What gave me strength and motivation during these phases was the belief that chaplains could work out of their own discipline of spiritual care (versus using primarily psychodynamic language or handling complaints about the church), and that it was our responsibility as professionally trained chaplains to develop the knowledge and tools in order to make substantive contributions to our own field.

A PASTORAL VISION AND METHODOLOGY FOR TUMULTUOUS TIMES IN HEALTH CARE

From the outset, pastoral care was always intended for patients, families and staff–not as possibly, separate recipients of care, but as a wholistic system containing the mutual interactions of care giving and receiving. In order to accomplish this, our departmental challenge at this time was for staff chaplains to start becoming fully integrated participants within interdisciplinary care teams in the direct care of patients, their support partners, and staff.

I offer this short history as background because, in my estimation, *The Discipline* is a community-based, cumulative, and collaborative pastoral vision. No one person formulated its creation. Its contributors were patients via their manifold experiences and the various clinical service line chaplains in the department who respectfully re-presented patients' sense of the Holy, Community, Meaning and Hope. For our hospital setting, these four elements seemed to be the key spiritual dynamics that patients were universally working with in order to struggle towards healing and full recovery. With the facilitation of the director who listened to our cumulative, interdisciplinary visits with patients and their support partners, we identified the patterns that we observed emerging from pastoral encounters. The pastoral-clinical approach and understandings of constitutive structures of *The Discipline* were born out of challenges to develop creativity and compassion for greater sensitivity to patients' spirituality: how does this person's spirituality function in the light of her or his illness, hospitalization and ability to return to her or his relationships with quality of life? The intent of such a question was not for the sake of pure analysis, but for how to be with a person in a covenant relationship that could draw upon spiritual resources–internal and external–for healing. This is why *The Disciple* starts with a person-centered basis of Needs, Hopes and Resources. Human beings are more than their needs; they are also about their hopes and resources, which include their spirituality, community, cultures, values and beliefs.

Personally, this approach led me to consider how people's spirituality actually functioned in regards to adjustments following open-heart surgery. It was both exciting and fretful to consider spirituality in this way–exciting to work with the vitalizing elements of a person's life and fretful in realizing the responsibility and integrity required for this kind of ministry. The most difficult part of working with *The Discipline* was relaxing with it and remembering that it was a means, a tool, and not the end or purpose of the visit. When I presented this difficulty to my director, he helped me find my sense of ease as I learned to wait and let the patient emerge as a person and as a presence. I quickly learned that it was not a substitute for developing pastoral rapport and relationship. The relational work was necessary and had to be done. Instead, *The Discipline* helped me to frame what I was witnessing about a patient as the person came forward with their meaning worlds always in play in the background. It became a way of perceiving what people were indicating in their narratives, what they wanted me to notice as I listened to their stories (Gerkin, 1984). *The Discipline* helped me receive each person in her or his struggles, dreams and endeavors. Also, it helped me see the landscape of a person's spirituality that could be tapped and made more visible as the person was becoming disappointed, disillusioned, despondent or despairing on the one hand and hopeful, making meaning, finding purpose and a foreseeable future on the other.

The unanticipated ways that *The Discipline* personally impacted me as a chaplain and my pastoral practice with patients occurred when I realized that I was being "eaten up" by trying to see as many patients as I could. Being consumed by activity that lessened how fully available I could be with patients, I worked with *The Discipline* enough to find a sufficient objectivity that ironically provided a distancing that actually allowed me to relax and afforded me to be closer and more available to patients in their narratives. I was amazed by this difference and how it worked, bringing about in me a presence that was truly pastoral. In time, I would engage the struggle around learning the difference between chaplain as role and chaplain as relationship. In a fundamental sense, the experience of being in the role came first; reflection and theorizing came later. Learning how "Needs, Hopes and Resources" worked in *The Discipline,* I became more aware of a pastoral approach for how people might "show up" in their spirituality and present themselves in the language of their own experiences. Later, when I became more conscious of myself as chaplain in relationship, I experienced that my openness to patients and the narratives that conveyed their life meanings was enhanced by having in the back of my mind a resilient template which fairly well illustrated what previous heart patients had been telling me–about what led to or hindered an envisioning of the future that they could welcome, manage and live into. Upon entering each new patient's room, I did not have to induce stupidity nor forgetfulness of other previous patients' experiences in order to be open and fully available to that patient. By using *The Discipline,* I was able to notice in more deliberative ways the significance and meaning of what patients were actually saying to me in the contexts of their hospitalization, surgery outcomes, and fears concerning their recovery efforts and future physical rehabilitation. It allowed me a spiritual lens whereby I could relax and receive the preciousness of what patients were entrusting to me, better understand its impact upon them by appreciating their spiritual struggles and the underlying dis-ease to their disease process.

In the blended narratives of their illness, social histories and personal experiences. I listened with them for the spiritual themes and interpersonal patterns of relating and communication. In wanting to work with the spirituality of each person, *The Discipline* afforded me a way to externally maximize each person's recovery from open-heart surgery by maximizing communication with the interdisciplinary team regarding how each patient was experiencing her or his recovery. I witnessed how they were experiencing their own recovery as they opened up what it was like to suffer from harsh life losses, to be unable to grieve, and to struggle with putting together a future that they desired. I became intensely aware of their lives before hospitalization and surgery, how all of this does not magically go away once patients come through the front doors of the hospital, and the perplexing question of how do people exactly get through their hospital stays intact and vertical? *The Discipline* helped me, not by providing answers, but in how to enter into the perplexities facing patients and viewing how they were shaping responses to their own predicaments when an interested enough person was willing to be with them. *The Discipline* actually helped provide that interest because I learned that although heart patients had similar behavior and religious cultural patterns, their expressions were multi-faceted and diverse. I was changed and fascinated by how people invited me into their deepest meanings when they were hurting and most vulnerable, never ceasing to be relational. My care practices as a chaplain changed as my work expanded into using *The Discipline* for family care support. Because I was better equipped to learn how patients' spiritual distress could be profiled, I had a working knowledge of how each patient's spirituality was negatively affected and shaped by her or his family system. Likewise, because I was equipped to profile dynamically how patients worked with their spirituality to heal and recover, I searched for positive factors in family systems that generated and supported thriving recovery. This work with families allowed me to become a strategic resource for family care.

Eventually, the healing team's care practices also changed as physicians and nurses contended with and included family care in their treatment of patients. For family support as well as patient care perceived as a whole system, doctors would request and incorporate the chaplain's understanding of patients' needs, hopes and resources; spiritual profile; outcomes; plan of care; interventions; and evaluation. It took me awhile to find the confidence, courage and competency to speak with the medical care team about patients' recovery. Essential to this development was first finding a relational attitude that would want me to develop language that was inclusive of physicians, nurses and ancillary support staff. I knew how medical terminology often had put people off, and I realized that spiritual language could also have the same effect on the interdisciplinary team. My department director helped me to realize two important lessons: First, that what I observed about patients and their support partners through the use of *The Discipline* could help the medical team give better, more intentional care. Secondly, *The Discipline* could help in patients' internal experience of their recovery. That is, sharing with patients what I was observing as chaplain might strengthen their motivation for healing so that they could work with and directly participate in their recovery. Therefore, chaplain's outcomes were contributory towards the larger team outcomes for patients. This kind of pastoral work involved concretely assisting patients and their support partners in how heart disease would impact and bring about changes to their future, their relationships and their desired lifestyles as well as providing support to them so that they could begin coping with these changes.

THE PROBLEMATIC OF A PASTORAL METHODOLOGY

To claim *The Discipline* as a pastoral methodology may seem, at first glance, to be a contradiction in terms. Many chaplains have received in their previous pastoral training the imperative that to be "pastoral" is to "attend to" or "wait upon" the patients or family members. This perception of the pastoral enters into the actual practice of chaplains as a caring presence willing to listen to what patients or family members might have to say. Such relationships understand pastoral presence as a making available the time and the space wherein patients and family members enjoy the freedom to cope in their own ways. For the chaplain not to offer this possibility can be understood as trespassing upon the sacred space of persons who often are emotionally vulnerable, physically weak or psychologically distressed. Therefore, to be professional in this paradigm may be interpreted as a deliberate and careful pastoral stance to not impose the chaplain's agenda, perspectives or interpretations upon ailing patient and/or family experiences. Such a pastoral model might view methodology as bad pastoral care in the least and as non-caring at its worst.

The theological rationale for such a model of pastoral care can best be described in Matthew Fox's words as "letting be: letting God be God, letting self be self, letting suffering be suffering, letting joy be joy" (Fox, 1990). This pastoral attitude of "letting be" is for the sake of reverence: it is considered not only a respectful approach of persons in their particular circumstances but also out of reverence for how God may be moving in a person's life. Not only is there carefulness that patients not be reduced to fitting the chaplains' pre-conceived categories or subjected to their interpretations, but also a caution that mysteries not be reduced to problems. Simply, let mysteries be! The underlying belief "to let things be" is to declare the holiness of all things. What chaplains are declaring in such a pastoral mode is that persons, as patients, and events need no changing by chaplains. Thereby, in the best understanding of this perspective, chaplains are affirming what the Creator first said: "It is good!" Fox further commentates: "It has something to teach us. I can be with it and learn, drink, take in, be nourished, be refreshed, be." "To do" would be viewed as driveness, activity for the purposes of manipulation. Such tampering would be considered a needless infringement upon persons.

The recent changes in health care policy and delivery have created a challenge and threat to conventional modalities of pastoral care. The reduction of chaplaincy staff or even elimination of entire pastoral care departments has created grave concerns concerning job security and fears for the future. The questions that emerge from such a crisis revolves around WHY: Why fix something that is not broken, or even considered by some as sacrosanct? Why something new? Why now? Why me? These very personal and professional concerns reach deep into chaplains' sense of identity, meaning and purpose. Chaplains feel coerced to change their ways of being chaplains in order to be in alignment with consumer market strategies, which come down from hospital administrators. Chaplains find themselves extricated from their familiar domains and stripped of their former privileges. Like strangers in alien territory, chaplains are challenged to (1) demonstrate to hospital and clinical leadership what they actually do; (2) produce clinical outcomes for their interventions and activity, and (3) make their accountability evident for the differences that chaplains make towards the overall care of patients and their families. Should these not transpire, their jobs might be in jeopardy at the hands of bean counters. It is no wonder, then, that the current turbulence in healthcare as an industry, particularly in a competitive market between non-profit and for-profit health systems, arouse tremendous passion in opposition to such trends. Feeling trapped and somewhat helpless by this wickedness, chaplains are outraged and suspicious; thoughts of Matthew 22: 17-22 enter the controversy–"Give ye to Caesar what belongs to Caesar and to God what belongs to God!" In this view, those chaplains who have chosen to work with and adapt to these trends are considered as having sold out to the enemy, not as innovators.

In the midst of such a prevailing climate enters a pastoral methodology such as *The Discipline*. Dualistic thinking possesses the power to split the solidarity and resolve of chaplains: are chaplains about being or doing? Regardless of one's stance, an alarming cry arises from our ranks: What can we DO ... to keep our jobs, to more strongly develop the profession of chaplains, and to be of greatest compassionate aid to persons who are suffering? Onto a scene, that already seems like a nightmare, can we really put our faith into something that appears to be devised by man? Particularly so, should that methodology seem, at first glance, to be mechanistic, one dimensionally flat and analytically sterile?

What I find intriguing in the pastoral approach of presence are the competencies that are actually exercised by chaplains when they are with patients: deep listening, acute wakefulness, and keen noticing are all implied in "letting be." This is certainly not an inactive pastoral stance. Instead, chaplains are increasingly refining their powers of observation that, in time, become integrated with their growing sense of vulnerability. These competencies, as combined into the craft and the art of chaplaincy, call for chaplains to be participating observers and observing participants. At this level of participation, as creativity and compassion become ways to spirituality, the persons in the pastoral encounter may be able "to experience what D.H. Lawrence calls 'at-ONE-met' and what theologians call 'grace'" (Fox, 1990).

Why would anyone want to change this picture? And what would a tool, like *The Discipline,* add to or enhance what chaplains are already doing?

What is currently being required of chaplains by healthcare leadership is structure, not content. Administrators want structure, structure that provides an overview of our content and even perhaps as a framework in order to "hold" or contain key dynamics that are operative in today's health care scene. And, here's the rub: the clinical settings where medical care is being practiced and pioneered are increasingly multi-disciplinary, multi-cultural, and multi-faith. These values in their different combinations can be considered contextual elements of a current, emerging pastoral vision–factors outside the normal domain of church attendance that shape and influence current understandings of state-of-the-art pastoral care.

STEPPING INTO THE LIGHT OF WHAT IS AT STAKE FOR CHAPLAINS

The scope of health care is so enormous that medical and nursing specialists work inside huge cradles of technical expertise and scientific knowledge that confound ordinary people. Within this context, the strong current of wholistic care appears with its ever-changing forms and understandings. Secondly, physicians are challenged in their medical practices to be sensitive to family care needs alongside individual patients' needs; having to work with intergenerational, family systems calls for a competence that works with diverse cultural contexts within a presenting phenomenon of a given family behavioral system. Thirdly, there now exists also a wider sense of global connections that represent a plurality of faith approaches that converge upon the local health care facility and impact both the ethos and ethics of care delivery. The accumulative consciousness of all these values–not just trends–and an intentionality to include them as standard care practices also impacts chaplains on the borderlands of their own professional practice. L. William Countryman (1999), an Episcopal priest and theologian, describes the borderlands experience in these terms:

> . . . It is a place of intense experience, not always pleasant. We may experience fear and dread, anger and desire in their full power. We are likely to encounter our own smallness and the limitations of our power in a way that proves, for a time at least, frightening. But we may also experience the love that binds

heaven and earth together, which pervades and unites all things. We may find a kind of joy that can only be described, in the language of absurdity, as ecstasy, an emerging from and standing outside oneself. We may experience a peace that is not absence of distress but rather an intense, intimate and fertile connection with oneself and one's world.

Regardless of where each of us is in health care today, chaplains can certainly identify with certain aspects, if not all, of what Countryman is describing. The external forces of quality assurance, customer satisfaction, and standards of excellence are powerful pressures weighing upon chaplains as much as they influence and demand change from other professional disciplines involved in direct patient care. At one level, we can perceive such commotion as threats that reach deep into our values and beliefs and rack our consciousness and motivations. Side-by-side on the same level, they challenge our creativity and compassion. We are challenged to be with people in the fullness of their humanity and spirituality when they are suffering and in pain within the very health care institutions where we, too, are suffering in the face of tumultuous changes. To where do these stirrings within and outside the soul lead us?

At this ponderous juncture, while we are still immersed in the previous question, we can now further ask: What is the point of such structures, such as *The Discipline,* for chaplains? Swinging between and within the space created by these two questions, our imaginations are able to perceive some interconnections, heretofore unseen at either end that may point towards directions of making an intuitive response.

The answer is what it has always been: person-centered care, but within a new understanding of what constitutes community and what it means to work within this new community of providing care where budgets are reality and honest dialogue is needed to collaboratively participate in problem resolution. As a professional community, chaplains are challenged to work within wider communities and interests that necessarily call forth a stretching and renewal of how we, individually but more importantly communally, understand our pastoral self, identity, theology and function.

In conclusion, *The Discipline* is a systematic, practical hermeneutical model of pastoral interaction which uses theological lenses and language for looking at personal and corporate experiences that deprive or give hope and/or meaning to a person's or community's actions or

---

existence. Its power comes from reflection on all levels of experience, that is, from the perspective of the personal experience and practice of patients or the experience and practice of the patient's community. This also entails description of personal religious experience, its institutional embodiment, and the special traditions from which it comes. Its content is theological and its scope is culturally sensitive. As such, *The Discipline* can also find valuable application in other than hospital settings, such as congregations and other non-medical settings.

REFERENCES

Countryman, L.W. (1999). *Living on the Border of the Holy: Renewing the Priesthood of All.* (Harrisburg: Morehouse Publishing), p. 11.

Fox, M. (1990). *A Spirituality Named Compassion.* (San Francisco: Harper & Row), pp. 90-91.

Gerkin, Charles V. (1984). *The Living Human Document.* (Nashville: Abingdon Press), pp. 26-28.

Whitehead, E.E. & Whitehead, J.D. (1982). *Community of Faith.* (Minneapolis: The Winston-Seabury Press), p. 153.

Living *The Discipline* on a Stem Cell Transplant Unit: Spiritual Care Outcomes Among Bone Marrow Transplant Survivors

Julie Allen Berger, DMin, BCC

SUMMARY. An oncology chaplain details, using *The Discipline for Pastoral Care Giving*, common themes in the spiritual journeys of stem cell/bone marrow transplantation survivors, and helpful chaplain interventions.

KEYWORDS. Oncology chaplain, interdisciplinary team, Discipline for Pastoral Care Giving, stem cell/bone marrow transplantation

A STORY

My introduction to the world of bone marrow transplantation (BMT) came from Ruby, a young mother of three I met in 1985, when transplants for leukemia were still relatively new in our medical center. Ruby taught me about the complex mix of needs, hopes, and resources that BMT patients bring to their transplant process. She was

Rev. Julie Allen Berger is Chaplain for Oncology Services, Barnes-Jewish Hospital at Washington University Medical Center, St. Louis, MO (E-mail: jab0539@ bjc.org).

far from her Louisiana home and had, just prior to her hospitalization for leukemia, been the primary caregiver for a daughter, also treated for cancer at a southern children's research hospital. Her daughter had recovered for the time being, but most of Ruby's extended family, including her husband, had to stay in Louisiana to care for the household while Ruby underwent experimental treatment at our Center. Ruby was often alone.

Some days Ruby was very focused on wondering how her family back home was faring. Other days, she was sharply reminded by her physical discomfort that she had to focus on herself and surviving the rigors of transplant. Some days she requested prayer and had little energy for visiting. Other days, she regaled me and other staff with tales of her exploits in our hospital community (Ruby helping her nurse "sweep" a mouse out of her hospital room was especially memorable).

I rejoiced with Ruby at the completion of her transplant and was naively unprepared for her ensuing return to the hospital, to die of problems related to graft-vs.-host disease (a common post-transplant phenomenon in which engrafted bone marrow rejects its host). I distinctly recall the day when I realized Ruby had laid aside concerns about her family's coping in the face of needing to reserve resources for her own dying process.

Fifteen years ago when I served as Ruby's chaplain, I was following patients at their own request for pastoral care. The world of BMT was new to me and I played no integrated role as a member of the BMT team. The twists and turns of Ruby's post-transplant complications (now so familiar) were a shock to me. I had no cumulative experience, no knowledge of how other transplant patients often coped with the unknowns in their future.

I believe I provided good spiritual care to Ruby by being present, helping her articulate losses, concerns, prayers and grounds for hope. However, remembering my relationship with this patient helps me realize how my care has evolved over the years, shaped by *The Discipline* or lens through which I now view both the oncology patient before me, and my opportunities as a clinically oriented chaplain.

INTRODUCTION

I chart some of the change in my identity as a clinical staff chaplain by remembering when it suddenly felt natural, rather than presumptive, to speak of how we as the BMT team were responding to particular patient needs. I was not naive to the BMT process anymore; I had grown into the oncology ministry and could speak with some precision about Spiritual Care's contributions to healing.

A lot of energy has recently gone into constructing pastoral "map-like" endeavors: *The Discipline* described in this volume, clinical pathways (Berger, 1998; Cusick, 1998; Handzo, 1998; Hilsman, 1998), indices (Yim & VandeCreek, 1996), and lately, spirituality screening tools for use with distinct clinical populations (Fitchett, 1999; Pargament et al., 1998). These instruments identify spiritual issues and coping styles of patients with similar diseases/ treatments as well as useful spiritual care interventions and outcomes. They all have the same destination: healing in the broadest sense and helping us "red-flag" spirituality styles which are less helpful (Pargament et al., 1998).

PURPOSE

Using *The Discipline,* this article describes: (1) commonalities among the spiritual journeys of stem cell/bone marrow transplantation survivors and (2) helpful chaplain interventions. I echo two of Chaplain Lucas' observations. There is a creative tension between the uniqueness and commonality of patients sharing a specific illness/ treatment challenge. Mrs. Jones, for example, will always have her unique spiritual story as well as being the typical "anxious, matched unrelated donor recipient in Bed 13," struggling like many before her. There is also a tension between chaplains' pastoral presence ("being") and "doing"–identifying and measuring outcomes. Chaplain John Gleason (1998) has written helpfully about the paradigm shift in professional chaplaincy from a Rogerian client-centered method to emerging standards of practice in assessing individual spiritual needs. My hope for this article is to help others learn from my ongoing "maturing" as an oncology chaplain, highlighting a way through the tensions between being and doing.

While not within the scope of this article, it is important to acknowledge the numerous losses and other crises that occur for most BMT patients prior to ever beginning their transplant. These include initial cancer diagnosis, previous treatment, news of recurrence, etc., as I have previously described (Berger, 1998). In retrospect, it seems that as the number of transplants performed in our Center has increased over the years, the oncology chaplain's interventions have more and more focused on those frequently hospitalized for post-transplant complications. It is this population I focus on in this article.

The majority of transplants in our Cancer Center are now peripheral blood stem cell transplants. Immature blood cells are harvested through pheresis and used because they grow faster after transplantation. I refer to the transplant experience in this article as "BMT" because the original procedure involved extraction of donor bone marrow and a longer recovery period for the recipient.

PSYCHOSOCIAL THEMES AMONG BMT SURVIVORS

The early nineties produced several good articles in the nursing literature about the psychosocial aspects of BMT experiences, including the work of Ferrell and her colleagues (1992) who examined the quality of life (QOL) for bone marrow transplant survivors. These researchers noted what I learned from Ruby and many others, namely that BMT survivors face not only acute demands of the transplant itself, but often a chronic post-transplant illness.

SPIRITUAL THEMES AMONG BMT SURVIVORS

In Ferrell's study (1992), 119 BMT survivors responded to mailed surveys that included the question, "What does Quality of Life mean to you?" These themes emerged, listed here in the order of how frequently they appeared:

1. Having Family and Relationships
2. Being Independent
3. Being Healthy (comments identified physical, mental, and spiritual health)
4. Being Able to Work/Financial Success
5. Having a Heightened Appreciation for Life
6. Being Alive
7. Being Satisfied/Fulfilled with Life
8. Being Normal.

I include the Ferrell study because its psychosocial concerns mirror spiritual themes I frequently hear. The survivors were also asked how they felt their transplant had affected their QOL. Their responses are paraphrased on the left-hand column of Figure 1. On the right-hand side of the figure, I have placed corresponding themes/questions that frequently appear in spiritual profiles when *The Discipline* is used as a lens.

FIGURE 1. QOL Survival Concerns/Corresponding Spiritual Themes

1. Side Effects	Is God still with me, especially when I'm not feeling like a valiant victor? Did I make the right decision, to go for BMT?
2. Infertility	What do I do with broken dreams/future stories? (Mourning losses). Can I still contribute to the future? What is God's intention for me?
3. Fear of Relapse	How can I find hope when my future is uncertain? What hopes propel me forward even if I don't have a long life ahead? Can I entrust my loved ones to God if I don't survive?
4. Decreased Strength/Stamina and 5. Work/Activities Limited	Can God's strength (not my body's) be mine for this recovery time? Will this period pass? Is there meaning in waiting? Can God enable me to accept new roles? Am I only a burden?
6. Second Chance	I'm "born again," physically and spiritually. I took a risk in faith and I've been rewarded.
7. My QOL Is Better	Even with complications, my life has been enriched by the transplant experience. I see life from a bigger, deeper, fresher perspective.
8. My Spirituality Increased	I feel (or want to feel) closer to God/loved ones. My understanding of who God is has broadened (or diminished, depending on the individual's perception of God's activity in the face of illness).
9. Greater Appreciation for Life	I've faced my mortality. I want to "give back."

SPIRITUAL CARE INTERVENTIONS/OUTCOMES CONTRIBUTED TOWARDS HEALING

A frequent theme of BMT patients is the guilt of "dragging loved ones through this with me," particularly among those with post-transplant complications. Chaplains make an important intervention when they help a survivor accept that love may include the suffering of loved ones on their behalf. Another important intervention invites patients to discover that one of God's gifts is receiving care instead of always giving it, particularly if their former role at home was primary nurturer. Finding ways of expressing anger towards God for not fixing everything becomes a critical outcome chaplains can facilitate with patients. This contributes towards their ability to retain God as an ally, albeit one who may have disappointed them.

A thorough spiritual assessment of patients during their transplant process becomes invaluable during post-transplant hospitalizations. The previously compiled (and charted) profile of spiritual resources and needs (e.g., faith learned as a child, current spiritual quest, questions illness has raised within a belief system) helps the chaplain to revisit the individual patient's toolkit of spiritual reflections. Are there some previously helpful beliefs or experiences of the Holy (even early in life) that can serve the patient now, during this period that feels like a significant step backward physically as well as spiritually?

A patient's failure to thrive post-BMT and fear of relapse often bring depression and spiritual distress. A cancer center with psychiatric/psychological support built into BMT treatment offers a prime opportunity for chaplain and clinical social worker/mental health professional to work as an integrated team. While counseling opportunities invite depressed/distressed patients to identify fears, losses and concerns, the chaplain provides time for patients to "check the temperature" of their faith life. Is an individual able to name something that makes surviving these uncomfortable and scary complications worth it? (*Hope*). Is the patient finding his/her image of God/a Higher Power adequate for this current struggle? (*Concept of the Holy*). Pastoral Counselor Jann Aldredge Clanton (1998) shares a wonderful vignette about encouraging a faithfully religious patient to forgive God for failed cancer treatment.

The spiritually distressed patient may test the chaplain to see if complaints about beliefs or faith community are tolerated. ("My church has let me down . . . those whom I thought would help haven't darkened the door.") While the chaplain validates this disappointment, patients can be invited to identify what has become their most helpful community . . . in some cases, it is the hospital staff itself (*Community*) (Steeves, 1992). Chaplains and mental health professionals can helpfully collaborate by encouraging patients to understand the meaning this illness (and its complications) has for them emotionally and spiritually (*Meaning*).

While many BMT survivors openly discuss their newfound appreciation for life post-transplant with evangelistic fervor, others may find they prefer to reflect privately with chaplains or clergy about how their view of life has changed. Especially with post-treatment complications, patients may do much second-guessing, wondering whether the risk of transplant was the right choice after all. Chaplain interventions here may include inviting patients to examine other life choices and God's perceived role in the midst of them. An outcome contributed towards healing may be an emerging sense of spiritual peace for the patient, about making the best decision possible at the time and entrusting an unknown future to God.

Many have written about the need of cancer patients to feel that they have contributed something to the human endeavor (Lester, 1995). Sometimes, in my experience, BMT survivors with complications get caught because they feel a special responsibility to remain heroes and not let their supporters down. They have understood their role as maintaining the faith, or the fight–not only to survive, but also to inspire others. At a time of spiritual or physical distress, they lose what they'd experienced up until now as a God-given role. They question the role and often feel guilty for disappointing others, even their physicians at times. A chaplain's intervention at this juncture may be to normalize spiritual doubts/questions as authentic expressions of faith, pointing to the patient's possible new role of truth-teller. (One of the reflections I find myself making most often in the face of a BMT survivor's death, is that he/she "told it as it was," considered a great compliment by the staff.) An outcome contributed towards healing may be that patients recognize and claim an important new role, one especially meaningful to caregivers. While families may find it difficult to hear patients acknowledge suffering and doubt, the staff can in supportive ways help them understand that the patient is most able to feel whole when speaking honestly.

A tension common to BMT survivors undergoing post-transplant complications is how much responsibility patients hold for healing. Patients in most transplant programs are urged to partner with their physicians, to take initiative as much as possible in exercising and eating, to think positively, and not wallow in self-pity. Many in oncology have written about the hidden barb in the "you can heal yourself" philosophy taken to its furthest extreme (Spiegel, 1993). BMT patients who "fail treatment" (a loaded phrase), relapse, or experience life-threatening complications may believe they are responsible for their failing health, due to not enough positive thinking or religious faith. A chaplain's intervention here can challenge patient beliefs that they have sole power to determine the future (God speaking out of the whirlwind to Job is a useful reference). Jann Aldredge-Clanton (1998) offers a story of inviting a cancer patient to recall a time when a life crisis resolved despite the patient's spiritual doubts. These patients are aided in realizing that good outcomes are not dependent on the certainty of religious beliefs.

A chaplain's incisive questions about the patient's role in healing and hope point out both the importance of the patient as active participant in healing, and the limits of an individual's ability to control the future. This can be a scary process. For BMT survivors, an important outcome is claiming one's God-given strengths and skills while releasing to God the waiting and the uncertainty. The chaplain and the faith communities of patients serve as reminders that God is present no matter what the future brings. Good coordination between chaplains and the clergy of patients, if available, can be enormously helpful here.

Accepting "the world can go on without me" is an important realization for post-BMT patients if death appears to be near. Chaplain interventions inviting patients to explore end-of-life concerns need little additional comment here. My experience is that dying BMT survivors struggle with three major concerns: (1) wanting relief from pain/weakness, (2) wanting peace about their BMT decision and its failure to bring health, and (3) needing to release loved ones to God's care. Addressing these concerns may contribute towards a sense of release about that which one cannot control, and a sense of ultimate hope (e.g., in an afterlife, ability to claim one's contributions in life, appreciation that life will continue through one's descendants or life achievements).

MEASUREMENT OF OUTCOMES

Chaplains often find this step the most anxiety producing! It involves observing behavioral patient indicators that some movement towards healing occurs after the chaplain's intervention. For example, Joe, a BMT survivor, is frustrated that complications still occur for him years after transplant. Hospitalized for shingles, he admits to feeling almost foolish for believing that his life had once again become normal. The chaplain invites this devout Catholic to voice his anger at God ("You've let me down, God, and now I'm letting down people at my job"). Two days later, the patient reports the chaplain conversation prompted him to have a "heart-to-heart" with his wife, followed by a "good long cry." The patient then describes feeling better physically and spiritually. This illustrates what George Fitchett

(1999) describes as a patient with good spiritual resources feeling temporarily overwhelmed.

In contrast, another patient with poor religious coping and few spiritual resources experienced a post-BMT relapse. In Fitchett's terms, he had an under-developed and negative spirituality. Formerly convicted and imprisoned for a crime, Charles was haunted by guilt that God could never forgive him for the wrong he'd done. He felt his recurrence was proof of God's disgust. The chaplains' interventions with him as a lifelong but not religiously active Christian were to recall scriptural stories about divine forgiveness. Stories about the Prodigal Son as well as the conversation between Jesus and the criminals on the cross were helpful.

Measuring the outcomes of these interventions is more difficult and sometimes subjective. The two chaplains involved with Charles observed his tearfully grasping their hands firmly during prayer. Asked whether he could experience any sense of God's open arms, Charles' reply was "I hope so." As he prepared to enter hospice care at a nursing home in his rural community, Charles gave the chaplains permission to talk with a local clergy person who could offer prayer support. In this instance, the attention of the chaplains to measurement led to this clergy contact that functioned as another intervention.

A WORD ABOUT BMT STAFF

What about staff care on a BMT unit? This topic deserves another article. Here I note two primary features of BMT staff spiritual profiles. The questions they wrestle with tend to be (1) How do we promote hope with our patients when we know the real possibility of poor quality of life, or death, after BMT? and (2) What comfort do we find in the face of witnessing our patients and their loved ones' suffering?

Helpful chaplain interventions with staff include noting/making time for those who exhibit signs of spiritual distress (e.g., anger, inappropriate comments to other patients, tearfulness, extra-ordinary cynicism). Simply acknowledging on a frequent basis the difficulty of this work appears to be meaningful to most oncology professionals. Chaplains can be truth tellers by recalling with staff the effectiveness of their ministry with patients and loved ones, even when suffering is not erased. They point out how staff members have valued patients and their family members by caring not only professionally but also personally. Noting with BMT staff that they are emotionally and spiri-tually moved by the preciousness, tenacity and yet frailty of human life may enable them to better experience divine compassion. Remind-ing staff that their caring has made a difference in their patients' sense of wholeness, even if death follows, is an intervention chaplains can-not make often enough. These examples underscore the interventions of chaplains that contribute towards healing of hospital staff members.

CONCLUSION

I have described spiritual profiles common among long-term BMT survivors, and chaplain interventions that contribute to patient and staff healing. While oriented towards a specific clinical population, hopefully this discussion demonstrates the helpfulness of a lens through which to view patient, family or staff members' spiritual needs/hopes/and resources. Perhaps readers will recognize new ways in which they can use *The Discipline* within their own ministry con-text.

REFERENCES

Aldredge-Clanton, J. (1998). *Counseling People with Cancer* (Louisville: Westmin-ster John Knox Press, 78-79.

Berger, J. (1998). Identifying Spiritual Landscapes Among Oncology Patients. *Chap-laincy Today*, 14(2), 15-21.

Cusick, J. (1998). Paths They Have Not Known: Ministry to Leukemia Patients Using Clinical Pathways. *Chaplaincy Today*, 14(2), 22-29.

Ferrell, B., Grant, M., Schmidt, G., Rhiner, M., Whitehead, C., Fonbuena, P., & Forman, S. (1992). The Meaning of Quality of Life for Bone Marrow Transplant Survivors. *Cancer Nursing* (Part 1), 15(3), 153-160; *Cancer Nursing* (Part 2), 15(4), 247-253.

Fitchett, G. (1999). Screening for Spiritual Risk. *Chaplaincy Today*, 15(1), 2-12.

Fitchett, G. (1999). Selected Resources for Screening for Spiritual Risk. *Chaplaincy Today*, 15(1), 13-26.

Gleason, J. (1998). An Emerging Paradigm in Professional Chaplaincy. *Chaplaincy Today*, 14(2), 9-14.

Handzo, G. (1998). An Integrated System for the Assessment and Treatment of Psychological Social, and Spiritual Distress. *Chaplaincy Today*, 14(2), 30-37.

Hilsman, G. (1998). A Spiritual Pathway for Prior Grief. *Chaplaincy Today*, 14(2), 38-41.

Lester, A. D. (1995). *Hope in Pastoral Care and Counseling* (Louisville: Westmin-ster John Knox Press).

Pargament, K., Zinnbauer, B., Scott, A., Butler, E., Zerowin, J., & Stanik, P. (1998). Red Flags and Religious Coping: Identifying Some Religious Warning Signs Among People in Crisis. *Journal of Clinical Psychology.* 54, 77-89.

Spiegel, D. (1993). *Living Beyond Limits,* (New York: Fawcett Columbine/Ballentine Books), 25.

Steeves, R. H. (1992). Patients Who Have Undergone Bone Marrow Transplantation: Their Quest for Meaning. *Oncology Nursing Forum,* 19(6), 899-905.

Wakefield, J., Cox, R. D., & Forrest, J. (1999). Seeds of Change: The development of a Spiritual Assessment Model. *Chaplaincy Today,* 15(1), 41-50.

Yim, R., & VandeCreek, L. (1996). Unbinding Grief and Life's Losses for Thriving Recovery After Open Heart Surgery. *The Caregiver Journal,* 12(2), 8-11.

A Disciplined Approach
to Spiritual Care Giving for Adults
Living with Cystic Fibrosis

Cheryl Palmer, MDiv, BCC

SUMMARY. Adults living with cystic fibrosis are less likely than other pulmonary patients to describe themselves as religious, to attend worship services regularly, to use god language, to describe their spiritual life, and in general, to give any obvious, outward indications of their spiritual strength, concerns, and depth. And yet, they have consistently demonstrated in chaplain-patient encounters an awareness of the function and importance of their spirituality in relation to life choices, coping with illness, facing mortality, and expressing life meaning, beliefs, and values. A disciplined approach by chaplains is a key component to engaging these patients so that each person's unique spiritual story unfolds. Results from *The Discipline* demonstrate how adults with cystic fibrosis are different in their expression and approach to spirituality from other pulmonary patients.

KEYWORDS. Chaplain, pastoral care, outcomes, interdisciplinary team, cystic fibrosis

If there is one mistake I have made as a chaplain, it is under-estimating the importance of spirituality in the lives of my patients. Perhaps this

Chaplain Cheryl Palmer is affiliated with the Barnes-Jewish Hospital Spiritual Care Services, One Barnes-Jewish Hospital Plaza, St. Louis, MO 63110 (E-Mail: clp1840@bjcmail.org).

sounds a bit ironic, but I continually marvel at how passionately patients will talk about their spirituality when given the opportunity. They eagerly describe their faith, beliefs, values, hopes, sense of life purpose, and other elements of their spirituality when chaplains demonstrate a genuine interest in understanding more clearly this part of their life.

Nowhere is this more evident than in my clinical chaplaincy with adults living with cystic fibrosis (CF). These patients, as a group, are the least traditionally religious patients I have within my pulmonary medicine and thoracic surgery clinical assignment. They are my least likely group of patients to describe themselves as religious, to attend worship services regularly (or even sporadically), to affiliate with a particular religious denomination, to use "god language" to describe their spiritual life, and in general, to give any obvious, outward signals of their spiritual strength, concerns, and depth.

And yet, my clinical experience is that adults living with CF engage me more deeply than any other patient group. Their concerns include questions about:

- Values (i.e., What is of ultimate importance to them?)
- Meaning (i.e., What does it mean to live with a chronic condition that likely could take their life?)
- Hope and Community (i.e., What and who keeps them going?)
- Mortality, Meaning, and Purpose (i.e., How can they deal with losses brought on by both their illness and normal life movements?)
- Purpose (i.e., What is their sense of life purpose?), and
- Relationship to the Holy or Other (i.e., What they believe about Something or Someone beyond themselves, about power, about miracles, about human suffering, about heaven or an afterlife, about dying, about living, and about healing.)

By what yardstick do I measure their spiritual intensity? It is their tenacity in seeking out the answers to their spiritual questions. It is their willingness to grapple with the uncertainty of spiritual doubt. It is their honesty in asserting what they truly believe, even if it is unconventional. There are no "pretenses" about the spirituality of these adults. They give it to you straight and honest.

CYSTIC FIBROSIS

CF is the most common inherited lethal disease among Caucasians in the United States although every race is affected by it. Approximately 30,000 people in the United States suffer from it and it occurs equally between both sexes. And today, because of enormous improvements in treatments, close to one-half of those with cystic fibrosis are adults. In 1991, the median survival age was 28 years; in the year 2000 it was 32.2 years. It affects the exocrine glands and causes progressive, multi-system disease, most notably chronic lung problems and pancreatic insufficiency.

The CF gene was initially identified in 1989 and has resulted in much treatment progress. Today, a child born with CF can expect to live a nearly normal life span. This is significant because most adults living with CF were virtually given a death sentence at birth. The parents were told their infant would likely not live more than one year.

These adult patients, therefore, have lived far beyond what was predicted and have had more than the usual amount of experience with the medical world. Growing up, it is common for these children to have had two hospital admissions yearly for management of their pulmonary symptoms. Daily life for both children and adults with cystic fibrosis consists of taking medications, doing chest physiotherapy, and eating nutritiously.

CF patients, family members, and friends have a real sense of community. Often, children and adults alike get to know one another through their regular hospital admissions and clinic visits. They keep up with one another outside the medical setting via telephone and activities together. They provide friendship, support, and understanding to each other as they share what it is like to live with this chronic condition.

Many have close calls with death. All know several friends who have already died with the disease. One 42-year-old patient told me that nine of his friends died in the previous year from CF and his disease had worsened to the point that he was being evaluated for lung transplant.

Is it any wonder then that these adults have a profound sensitivity to the spiritual dimension? I will never forget the 26-year-old woman who sat down in my office for our spiritual counseling session and stated: "I believe God is all-loving but I don't believe God is all-powerful." Her CF had progressed to end stage and her older sister had died of the same disease four years earlier. Questions of omnipotence, theodicy, meaning, purpose, and hope are often at the center of these pastoral encounters.

Another young man was struggling with living his life the way he believed was right for him instead of the way his wife and mother wanted him to live. He felt incredible conflict about living out his life's dreams and ambitions because he felt so burdened with pleasing these persons who had done so much for him. He came to me because of the moral conflict he felt in not following what he felt was right for him. He was never able to make peace with himself and died one year after we met. My grief was all the more intense knowing he hid his true self from those closest to him.

So in spite of their lack of affiliation with traditional religion or of participation in worship services, adults with CF more than any other group of patients in my clinical practice, demonstrate a keen interest in exploring their spiritual life with me. Another evidence of this phenomenon is that these patients, more than any other, seek me out in my office for private spiritual counsel about the above enumerated spiritual issues and/or request me to stop by to see them when they are admitted to the hospital. Certainly, every adult living with cystic fibrosis is not like this, but more often than not, they are open to spiritual care giving offered by the chaplain.

THE DISCIPLINED APPROACH

So, what made me notice the deep spirituality of adults living with CF? The key has been a disciplined approach to providing spiritual care not only to those living with CF, but to all of my patients. When I use the terms "disciplined approach," I mean that:

- There is a relationship priority between the patient and myself. The foundation of *The Discipline* is establishing a trusting pastoral relationship with the patient.
- There is a clear sense of purpose as to why I'm there. *The Discipline* begins with rapport building and spiritual assessment. From there, outcomes and a suitable spiritual care plan are developed with the patient. So when I return to the patient, the visit is related, along with its interventions, to the outcomes and plan we have established. Depending upon what the hoped for outcomes are, the visit may focus on providing religious rituals, prayer, discussing the meaning of losses and changes in the patient's life, exploring what it means to feel doubt and a whole range of spiri-

tual issues, questions, and interventions. Of course, other issues may arise and are addressed as is appropriate. The spiritual care plan is modified accordingly.

• There is a professional focus on how this person's spirituality is functioning today in the context of their life history and current condition so that my spiritual care may be customized to this individual today.

Why has *The Discipline* made a difference in my clinical practice and understanding of the unique features of my patients' spiritual journeys? Very simply, this approach breaks down my multiple patient encounters into components I can examine, reflect upon, compare and contrast, observe for trends, learn from, and apply to my ministry with each of my patients. An important benefit to the disciplined approach to spiritual care giving is the capacity to compare and contrast various patients and 'to note trends among patient groups. An example from my clinical practice will demonstrate the benefit of a disciplined approach to spiritual care giving.

SPIRITUAL CARE TO LUNG TRANSPLANT AND CF PATIENTS

Lung transplant patients were the first large patient group with whom I applied *The Discipline*. As described in an earlier article (Palmer & VandeCreek, 1996):

> The beginnings of investigation into the spiritual needs and resources of lung transplant patients . . . were practical. We sought a disciplined, reliable way to report to a multidisciplinary team about the role and importance of each person's spirituality in dealing with the transplant process. The goal was to report how Patients' religious affiliation, faith practices, beliefs, values, understanding of life purpose, understanding of illness and where they gained hope, contributed to both their well-being and coping capabilities. A second goal was to develop a tailor-made spiritual care plan so that the patients gained maximum benefit from the lung transplant, and individual spiritual practices and beliefs were respected.

Among the disease processes that lead to end stage lung disease is CF. So among the patients coming for lung transplantation in this study were adults with CF (19% of the patient mix). Other diagnoses included: chronic obstructive pulmonary disease including alpha I antitrypsin deficiency, emphysema, and chronic bronchitis (46%), primary pulmonary hypertension (14%), pulmonary fibrosis (12%) and miscellaneous pulmonary diagnoses (9%). There were 111 participants in the study group.

The disciplined process I developed for this group of patients included: an initial semi-structured pastoral interview, a written Spiritual Assessment Profile, and the development of a customized spiritual care giving plan for each patient as he or she went through the lung transplant process of waiting for their transplant, having their transplant, and developing a spiritual care discharge plan to home to enhance their life after receiving a lung transplant. The spiritual care plan, of course, was continually modified as needed.

Key elements examined with each patient included their sense of the Holy or God, their sense of meaning especially in the context of their illness and what they were going through, and their sense of life purpose and direction. I also inquired concerning the people they could count on in their community, in whom or what did they hope, and what were the important spiritual and faith practices in their life.

Many chaplains react with surprise when they see the depth of the spiritual assessment. Some wonder if patients balk at such "personal questions." My experience is that after I establish a trusting relationship, communicate my genuine interest in understanding how their spirituality functions, and that I intend to remain faithful in my relationship with them, most patients eagerly talk about what really matters in their lives. As a matter of fact, I often get the impression people are waiting for someone to ask about what they believe, what is of ultimate importance to them, what meaning they are drawing from this experience, how it might impact their life, and to offer to sojourn with them through this often frightful, new, uncharted experience. I believe that a deep need exists among all of us to be understood and loved for who we are. When that happens, we find courage, hope, and strength.

This disciplined approach to spiritual care giving was my first look at the unique features of the spirituality of adults living with CF. One of the real coping strengths of these adults is their capacity to form trusting relationships with members of their health care team. After more than 10 years of experience in working with them, I now know much of the credit for this coping skill belongs to the groundwork laid by the pediatric CF team that encourages openness and partnership between the patient and team members. This ability to trust and create partnerships particularly has an impact on their sense of community and connection. The spiritual impact is both one of being valued and a steady sense of hopefulness.

Particularly significant is that CF persons constitute an outlier group among other lung transplant patients. As a group, they tend to be unmarried, with no formal religious affiliation. Both of these factors are associated with lower religious and spiritual well-being scores when compared to the lung transplant group. However, my continuing encounters clearly demonstrate the presence of considerable spiritual resources.

Thus, *The Discipline* provides opportunities to compare and contrast groups of patients, better understand the substance behind the differences, and to provide spiritual care plans tailored to particular patient's needs, hopes, and resources. Over time, these initial results have been further confirmed with CF adults who are not necessarily interested in or candidates for lung transplantation.

TEAM OPENNESS AND INTEGRATION

This disciplined approach to spiritual care opened the door for me to become a member of the first Adult CF Team at this medical center in 1993. In the early 1990's, children with CF were living into young adulthood and a decision was made to transition these adult patients to adult pulmonologists. Most of the first members of this new team were associated with the Lung Transplant Team, largely because that was one of the few places in our adult hospital where there were experienced professionals. Since I had worked with these professionals since 1989, I naturally became a team member along with the social worker, the dietician, and a physician.

While I was at the right place at the right time, I also contend that the opportunity to join the Team was a result of their appreciation of spiritual care as a routine part of patient care similar to addressing nutrition issues, social issues, physical therapy issues and the wide variety of issues their patients face. My colleagues had come to see the value of knowing how patient's core beliefs, ultimate values, and hopes affected coping, decision-making style, and how the patient's spiritual resources might help in adjusting to changes (both good and bad) in their life. They understood the value of attending to spiritual concerns because it improved patient well-being and satisfaction. Spiritual care giving was, thus, *contributing* to the overall clinical outcomes, helping patients resume normal activities of daily life.

Moreover, they saw the chaplain as the appropriate professional to assess spiritual needs, resources, and hopes and to develop an approach to spiritual care giving. I am convinced the disciplined approach enabled me to communicate in a consistent, reliable, and understandable way about the spiritual dimension so that my colleagues could see spiritual care as essential rather than as just something "nice." Thus, there is a standing order that the chaplain provides spiritual assessment and care for all adult CF patients. I meet weekly with the team to discuss patients both in-house and those seen in the clinic. And, I have had the privilege of addressing the International Cystic Fibrosis Annual Meeting (1997) on the topic of spirituality among adults living with this disease. Not only is there openness among my colleagues, but deep respect and valuing of spiritual care giving.

In summary, the integration of spiritual care into the overall care plans of patients and having it recognized as a contributing discipline to overall clinical outcomes has occurred over a long period of time. It has also come in a clinical area where I initially found physicians, nurses, social workers, psychologists, and other members of the treatment team open to adding the chaplain to the team. One of my guiding principles is to go where the door is most open. My second principle is to de-mystify what I do and speak plainly about how faith and/or spirituality functions in patients' lives. The third principle is to be consistent and reliable in what I do. And, finally, I remind myself that the job of educating never ends. Together, these elements have enriched my ministry with my patients.

REFERENCE

Palmer, Cheryl & VandeCreek, Larry. (1996). Religious Evaluation of Lung Transplant Patients. *The Caregiver Journal, 12 (3)*, 9-19.

The Discipline:
A Pastoral Care Methodology with Violent Victims of Violence

Lawrence Olatunde, MDiv

SUMMARY. Ours is a violent culture and violence creates victims. Many of these victims are themselves violent. This article describes *The Discipline* as used in the pastoral care process that seeks to rehabilitate these violent victims. The process involves 5 Rs: Rapport, Reflection, Realization, Reorientation, and Reintegration.

KEYWORDS. Chaplain, pastoral care, outcomes, interdisciplinary team, violence victims, religiosity, change

Violence is a major epidemic in our society. Murder is the leading cause of death among African American teenagers. One out of every four African American males is likely to be in prison or dead by the age of twenty-one. Inner cities are the war zones of urban America, consumed by drugs, gang violence, rape, and robbery. And, recent shootings in the schools show that violence is no longer limited to the inner cities.

Where there is crime, there are victims and society will react. Reactions include:

Lawrence Olatunde is affiliated with the Barnes-Jewish Hospital Spiritual Care Services, One Barnes-Jewish Hospital Plaza, St. Louis, MO 63110 (E-mail: loo8205@bjc.org).

- The fear of living in the inner cities that results in massive immigration to suburban areas. Senseless violent activities encourage people to flee as far as they can from the inner city.
- Neighborhood Watch: Some communities develop neighborhood watch, from which the idea of "not in my backyard" has emerged.
- Political Focus: Crime continues to be a dominant political issue in presidential campaigns.
- More Prison Facilities: In the recent years, this emphasis on more prisons constitutes an effort to remove criminals from the society, hoping that getting rid of "bad guys" will bring peace.
- New Legislation: The "three strikes and you're out" policy is an emphatic reaction to violence. It is another form of banishing criminals from the society.
- More Police Officers: The increase of one hundred thousand police officers on the streets in America is an attempt to reduce the epidemic at all cost.

These are indications that everyone is tired, scared, and wants an effective solution to the epidemic. Unfortunately, violence does not seem to stop.

TAKING A CLOSER LOOK AT THE PROBLEM

The medical center in which I provide ministry includes the larger and busier of two Level I trauma centers in the city of St. Louis, Missouri. As such, the Emergency Department receives approximately 2,500 victims of violence each year.

Having specialized in Emergency & Trauma Services Chaplaincy since 1995, I continue to be moved by the victims of violence, especially those whom we began to speak of as "violent victims of violence" (VVOV). They come to us for care as victims of violence in their own right. They have been shot, stabbed, raped, beaten, or victimized in some other way by street violence (as opposed to domestic violence). On another night or on another street, they are also men and women who might be violently victimizing someone else. They tend to be men and women caught up in a life that has violence as an integral part.

I committed myself to better understanding what was involved in effective pastoral care for them. I spent two years studying their behavior, needs, hopes and resources. Developing an effective philosophy of pastoral care required a thorough understanding of their behavior and their worldview. During those years, I noticed that some had accepted pain and suffering as a way of life. They had seen their friends, siblings and neighbors killed or badly wounded. Many already presume themselves to be dead. Dykstra (1997) quotes one VVOV as saying,

> I am not afraid of death. You could put a gun to my head, I wouldn't be afraid of death. I am already dead.

For most of these individuals, the parents are very scared; day after day they worry about their family members. They wish for a change of behavior but they do not know what to do, whom to trust, or who is truly interested in them. Many VVOVs are regarded as outcasts and troublemakers in their communities. Thus, they find it difficult to trust anybody. I, along with many others, believe that trying to heal the wounds through modern medicine, praying and preaching is not sufficient to accomplish the needed changes. Facilitating the required level of healing requires a very disciplined, well constructed, and persistent methodology to deal with these patients if the epidemic is to be moderated. Contributing factors must be identified in order to design models that will provide effective spiritual care to this population.

CONTRIBUTING FACTORS TO VIOLENT ACTIVITIES

One of the major contributions to violent activities is the fact that many VVOVs often see themselves primarily as victims. In contrast, unless careful attention is given to the issue, most health care providers do not see an attacker ("shooter," "dealer" or "banger") as a victim. R.X. is a 27-year-old male who was admitted for multiple gun shot wounds. Prior to this admission, he knew many of the trauma staff people at the hospital because he had been admitted for the same reason many times. A few weeks later, while I was helping him figure out his past, he said in frustration and anger:

> When you come to my neighborhood and all you can find from ghetto to ghetto are drugs, gangsters, alcoholism, prostitution, stealing, fathers in jail, mothers on drugs, teen pregnancies, most

kids dropping out of schools; when a person sees no alternative lifestyle but all this mess, then you will understand why I am a victim of this crazy America.

A closer look at the experiences of many VVOVs reveals that they are right in claiming to be victims. I have found understanding family systems and triangulation helpful in analyzing their situations. The first side of the triangle represents the victim, the second represents the perpetrator and the third represents the Rescuer. In the cases of most of the perpetrators of violence, many were born into dysfunctional families. Fathers were totally absent from their lives, unknown, imprisoned, unemployed or homeless. Mothers were having all kinds of financial crises, unemployed or barely making a minimum income. Some parents had drug and other kinds of social problems. The children born in such environments often lack basic human, person-to-person nourishment. When such nourishment is missing in people's lives, the children become victims, their parents actively or passively the perpetrators of the afflictions. Many VVOVs testify that looking for something to temporarily liberate them from these dilemmas has always been the only solution they could think of. One day a VVOV said to me:

> When you are going through such problems, you've got to do something. Many people think you're stupid, but you know you aren't. You know there is something you can do for yourself.

I observed many VVOVs reaching out, looking for solidarity and affection they missed at home and as young adults. In their search, they join others in similar situations, forming alliances so strong that they are willing to die for each other. The basic reason for such alliances among gang members is to experience relationships on which they can really count. Such solidarities, however, often lead to disruptive and disrespectful behavior at school and this results in their becoming outcasts. They are "the troublemakers" in the neighborhoods, breaking into homes, selling drugs, stealing, and committing all kinds of crimes until they end up in hospital beds, jails or morgues.

Historically, the methods used by females tend to be different from the males. They include reaching out to boyfriends, getting pregnant, having babies that they can love (i.e., hold on to), dropping out of school, ending up on welfare, and sometimes attempting suicide.

These are common female responses to the crises of their home and community. Increasingly, however, young women are choosing some of the same behavior and risks, with the same consequences, as the young men.

When such a life of violence continues, many of the VVOVs end up on probation, in prison, homeless, seriously injured or dead. The only institutions that they see as helpful (perhaps only temporarily helpful) are the hospitals. No other institution is designed for making the VVOVs feel better except the health care institutions. When VVOVs are on probation, they see themselves as the victims of the officers. When they are sent to prison, they see themselves as victims of "the system"; they may become worse criminals because of exposure to even more violent offenders. Hospitals are the only institutions to which they are generally willing to go and which exist for the purpose of saving their lives. Therefore, hospitals have a unique opportunity to help them with their problems. Unfortunately, many hospitals, like many other social institutions, fail to recognize the origin of the problem, focusing only on symptoms.

Working with VVOVs can be extremely difficult and even dangerous, yet professional chaplains are in unique positions to make a significant impact in their lives, even more so than the rest of the care team. As chaplains, what can we offer to the VVOVs? And how can we contribute to their care with some definite contributing outcomes? The aim of this paper is to present the spiritual care methodology with these patients that I have developed in almost five years of clinical experience. I acknowledge the help of Chaplain Art Lucas, Director of Spiritual Care Department at Barnes-Jewish Hospital, and Barry Hong, Ph.D., Medical Psychologist. Dr. Hong has helped me examine the demographic and religious variables of VVOVs and we will report our work together elsewhere.

WHO ARE THE VVOVs?

There are two types of victims of violence. First are the innocent victims. These are victims of robbery, random violence, drive by shooting, and mistaken identity who contribute nothing to the circumstances surrounding their violent experience. The second type consists of those who live lives of violence and become victims in the process. They may have hurt or killed someone before and are now the objects of revenge. They may become victims as a result of drug dealing, gang activities or robbery. These individuals actively participate in the causes that make them victims.

According to our data, 62 percent of the subjects promise to seek revenge on their attackers. More than half (62%) believe that they will be violently attacked again. Interestingly, about 40 percent openly express ownership of having contributed to their current violent experiences. When reporting contributing factors to the attack, the reasons include drug related issues, gang membership, robbery, romance disputes, etc.

The study also shows that virtually all VVOVs were, by their own report, meaningfully connected to religious groups early in life. Later, most of them had some negative experiences in their faith communities and virtually none were connected with or felt a part of faith communities when hospitalized as a VVOV. A large majority (98%) of the perpetrators were, in their own estimation, once meaningfully connected with a religious group in their childhood. Virtually all of them grew up in and felt loved by at least some in their faith groups. Some, however, experienced the church as too judgmental and full of condemnation.

Many are gang members and they learn to distrust everyone, regarding those outside their group as enemies. Therefore, regardless of good motives and interest in VVOVs, chaplains must earn their trust. They must prove that they care and have a genuine interest in them.

THE METHODOLOGY: 5 Rs

This methodology is designed to help the VVOVs achieve two goals, namely to *de-construct* their current lifestyles of violence, and second, to *reconstruct* a new lifestyle. In order to achieve these goals, victims are individually facilitated through five stages, the "5 Rs" of the methodology. Listed in their sequential order, they include:

- Rapport
- Reflection
- Realization
- Reorientation
- Reintegration.

STAGE ONE: RAPPORT

In this step, three preliminary considerations are important. First, a relational gap exists between VVOVs and the chaplains. Second, the hearts of VVOVs are yearning for love just like everybody else even though they may not act like it. Third, most VVOVs have the potential to change. Chaplains must see them for what they can become rather than for what they currently are.

Working with the VVOV must begin with developing good rapport. Failing to develop a good rapport during the initial stage spells failure for the rest of the stages. Offering anything before building a bridge between the victims and the chaplain will mean nothing, be ineffective and rigorously rejected. In order to develop good rapport, the chaplain must realize some of the causes for the relational gap.

How can rapport be established when their histories are often so different from most chaplains? The first key is patience. Building rapport requires time. Impatiently pushing ahead to the next goal in an ascribed time frame will fail. And, there will be many frustrations. Chaplains can do their best and see no effects for a long time.

The second key is empathy. Often this arises from chaplains recognizing their own woundedness and that they are now wounded healers. Having the gift and skill to hear and empathize their pain, being committed enough to join them in their pain, and being willing to be patient and take time until they are ready to respond positively are all simply required every time.

During the first few visits, the chaplains must develop, continuously test, and refine a good spiritual assessment. What can fill the gap between the chaplain and VVOVs? Some may honestly solicit and expect answers to their question, "Why am I still here?" This is often an honest question and their way of establishing companionship. To others, their clergy used to provide answers to all their questions and they expect the chaplain to do the same. Even as they raise questions, VVOVs may be hoping that your response will hint what sort of companionship you have to offer. In their responses, they will reveal what they consider to be important, what values and beliefs about life they use to make sense of their experiences. What kind of responses to the "Why me?" question do they consider? Do they reflect a rigid world of moral cause and effect where the violence that has happened to them is directly related to their bad behavior? Do they reflect a world built on power? What is the basis for power: number of friends, position, race, gun, right, force? What role do they expect you to play when those kinds of feelings and life questions are expressed? Do they, without even thinking about it, assume that you are there to condemn, or pronounce the truth, or be a nice guy, or do their bidding? VVOVs make all that material, and more, available to you in a typical conversation and it is important for an adequate spiritual assessment.

Chaplains must provide good listening ears as they express their frustrations, state of helplessness, and sense of loneliness in the midst of their pain. Believe the feelings and perspectives you hear. Allow the victim to set an agenda for dialogue even when chaplains feel that time is wasted. For example, some of VVOVs may want to talk about sports. Others may be interested in current affairs. At times some of their questions may be a test of the caregiver's commitment. One VVOV called for me one day. Unfortunately it was on my day off. The on-call chaplain went to see him. In spite of our well-established relationship, he did not trust the on-call chaplain. Testing the chaplain, he asked her to call his mother and made other seemingly small requests. Being under "a protective status," VVOVs generally do not have access to telephones. Although the chaplain tried to respond to his needs, he still noticed her uncomfortableness with his requests. When I went to see him upon my return to the hospital, he said:

> I couldn't talk to the other chaplain, man. Hey man, I can't even trust her with very simple stuff that an ordinary person can do for you. Hey man, how can I discuss anything else with that dude? I almost fooled myself, man, because I think all chaplains will be like you.

In order to bridge the gap the chaplain needs to realize that a violent act had been committed, and the patient is the victim in this case. The chaplain needs to be willing to show anger toward the perpetrator(s) and sympathize with the victim so that they know that the chaplain is on their side right now. Remember, this does not mean approval of their actions. Listening to their stories without criticism is another way of letting them know that the chaplain is on their side. Accept their story, even when it does not seem to add up. Most VVOVs change their story after good rapport is established. Chaplains need to tolerate both their own anger and the anger of VVOVs. By this, chaplains present themselves as the victim's allies and companion. Respecting them, showing them that they are seen with a sense of worth and of great value is another way of bridging the gap. This often paves the way for letting the victim see a need for an alternative lifestyle. The chaplain may well be treating them with respect in ways no one else has shown before.

How long can it take to build a good rapport with VVOVs? There is no definite answer to this question. No timetable can be set for achieving the goal. For some, loneliness helps them to trust more quickly. However, I have found some of the VVOVs whose families are Jehovah's Witnesses to be extremely slow to trust and to present unique challenges. It seems to take extra time for them to accept that the chaplain's intention is not to convert the victim to another belief.

STAGE TWO: REFLECTION

Since many victims became objects of condemnations, how can they be helped to even consider embracing new life? How can the chaplain help them without jeopardizing the relationship just established? How can this be done without afflicting the afflicted? The contributing outcome of this stage is to help the individuals through a time of reflection, allowing them to use their own mirrors to see themselves as they really are without pointing fingers of condemnation. The intent is to help them see a need for de-constructing their current life style and reconstructing a better one.

Most people live their lives without reflecting on them. Many follow thoughtless daily routines such as getting up in the morning and rushing to the bathroom, worrying about traffic on the way to work, or looking forward to lunch time. At the end of the day, they drive through traffic back home, have dinner with family or friends, go to a movie, or end the day by going to bed. This routine could be repeated throughout a lifetime without reflecting on it. For the hospitalized VVOVs, the regular circle is broken. Contact with the outside world is broken. If they are gang members, they are now disconnected and isolated from the gang. They are now patients in the hospital without their usual identities; usually their names do not even appear in hospital computers. They are the patients without telephones in their rooms and limited to very few visitors. These conditions are intended to protect them during their hospital stay, but they may experience it very differently. During these depressing, lonely and painful circumstances, the victims have plenty of opportunities to reflect on their lives. How can chaplains build on the opportunity to facilitate significant contributions for their lives? Here it is important to embrace the behavioral sciences as a partner to theology, contrary to Peterson's (1980, p. 138) narrow view of clinical pastoral training. Peterson described chaplains in hospitals as inferior members of multi-disciplinary teams. Making use of psychological tools is an advantage in dealing with victims of violence at this stage.

In order to help victims engage in helpful reflection, chaplains must be clear that the goal is not to condemn them but to allow them to see themselves, find what is wrong with their lives in their own terms, so that the reflections may result in personal conviction. This stage may take more time for some VVOVs than the other stages. Thus patience, again, is needed as chaplains gently help them through this process.

What they need to reflect on includes:

- family make up,
- social life, and
- spiritual life.

As regards family make up, they are asked to think about their lives as far back as they can remember. They start by thinking about their relationship to their parents. Which of their parents were more influential in their lives? Is there any particular lesson they remember learning from their parents? They carefully think about every member of their family. Which of them can be considered to be living a good life? What do they consider a good life or what a good life looks like? What contributes to such a good life? Which school did they attend and what is their educational level? Who are the most influential people in their lives?

Attention to their social life involves reflection on the neighborhood where they grew up, enabling them to talk about people who have influenced them. Reflecting on their friends, they can list column by column those who make positive and negative contributions to their lives. What kind of friends did they have? What were the levels of their education?

To reflect on their spiritual life, they usually start with thinking about their childhood faith communities. They think about what was going on when they stopped going to religious gatherings. Why did they stop? Who made an effort to reach out to them? When did they realize that life began to change for them? All these questions are just a few ways to lead or invite victims into their reflections.

During this stage each issue is dealt with before going to the next. Based on the chaplain's assessment of each individual, a variety of possibilities exist. For example, a person may become a victim as a result of sibling associations with gangsters. In such a case, chaplains need to find out more about the sibling. Is she or he still around? Or has she or he been sent out of town? How much influence does the sibling have on the VVOV? If the sibling is still around, the chaplain needs to spend time with such siblings. For instance, the chaplain may need to assess the level of his commitment to a gang, now that his brother has been hurt. Is he even more determined to get revenge? Does he appear to be indifferent about what has happened to his brother? Had he been hurt because of the VVOV's actions in the past? Does he feel remorse, regretful or confusion? Does he feel trapped and want to find a way out but scared of the gang's possible reactions? The assessment should lead to clearer directions and plans of reflections for both the VVOV and such sibling. In other cases, victims might have benefited from the illegal lifestyle of a family member, e.g., selling drugs. Such a case requires a different approach. How did the sibling arrive at this junction? How is the patient involved in such life style? How does he feel or react to this life style? Are there other sources for income or support for the hospitalized VVOV? In some cases, victims may blame and hate close family members for their suffering. The chaplain must try to find out exactly what the victim is talking about and help him work through his anger before moving forward. In some rare cases, the VVOV's family may feel indebted to the victim because they have helped put food on the table by selling drugs. Different issues need to be dealt with accordingly.

These sample questions and alternatives are intended to suggest how chaplains can facilitate this reflection in ways that do not push victims to defend their past. It needs to be done in ways that lead them to reach their own evaluation about their life. This reflection process, owned by VVOVs, must be in place before moving on.

STAGE THREE: REALIZATION

This is a crucial stage in the relationship. Here previous labors can begin to bear fruit or everything can be forfeited. Victims are examining their lives without anyone telling them how bad they have been, how many people they have hurt or killed, and what kind of punishment they deserve. By reflection, they have used their own mirrors to see more clearly what is wrong and right with their life styles. They often identify people who have made negative contributions to their lives and how family and friends have led them astray. For those from Christian families, they might remember participation in Sunday school or children's church. Some may remember good grades when they started school and how peer pressure led them to drop out of school and begin to live a criminal life. Some may be able to realize how many people they have hurt and what kind of punishment they think they deserve.

These reflections often lead to two possible reactions.

- *Anger and Depression*: This reaction can sometimes lead to suicide. "How could I allow this to happen to me?" It can also involve the casting of blame: "Why did my family let this happen to me?" It can also lead to hopelessness, realizing that they have gone too far. At this junction, a professional chaplain should engage other professional disciplines as necessary.
- *Desire for Life Change*: When individuals clearly see their lives as bad and desperate, they can be strongly motivated to do something about it. This desire for lifestyle change is the chaplain's contribution to an important outcome, one that may never be reached by many years of imprisonment.

At this stage, the VVOV is more active than the chaplain. However, chaplains need to be aware of and be prepared for any possible reactions. For example, most families will be thrilled about a positive realization by the VVOV because they wanted changes to occur. Others, however, may not be happy. The victims' criminal life may be the only source of sustenance for family members and they may actively discourage trusting the chaplain. They may try to justify the lifestyle by saying, "He is not a bad person, he loves to help people, he doesn't need a counselor." They often try to influence the patient to see the chaplain as "a bad guy" while projecting themselves as the patient's messiah. As is evident, these can be dangerous situations for chaplains.

STAGE FOUR: REORIENTATION

Realizing that something is wrong with one's life is only the beginning of change. The contributing outcome of this stage is helping victims accept some level of responsibility and to begin repairing the damage. This stage gives the chaplain an opportunity to help the individual de-construct the old life and reconstruct a new one.

In order to construct a new life, any valuable treasures from the old life need to be salvaged. The chaplain again takes issues one by one and deals with them until each one is examined and the implications for the future concretized. For instance, upon discharge from the hospital, there is often a need for temporary, safe relocation. Chaplains need to work with social workers to find a temporary suitable residence. There is always a need for new friends due to loneliness and isolation from former friends. The role of big brothers and sisters is very important here. Chaplains need to prepare those big brothers and sisters on how to encourage VVOVs and should facilitate their connections. Some victims may wish to return to school to earn a GED and this often requires tutors.

Chaplains need to clarify the VVOV's aspirations. For example, he may want to be a nurse, a police officer, or a counselor. What steps are required and is the individual ready to take them right now? The chaplain can help facilitate those steps. Another common need is drug treatment and rehabilitation. This stage is often the place to refer the VVOV to other professionals and local agencies for following up. No matter what happens during this stage, it must be wisely done so that a chaplain does not betray the victim's trust. Chaplains need to prepare them for such a transition and facilitate it, staying in touch with the victim so that the victim can move into the next stage.

STAGE FIVE: REINTEGRATION

This stage is probably the easiest. The victim has found in the chaplain a compassionate companion through a difficult journey. The relationship was a context for change. The dawn of the new life appears and progress is being made in rehabilitation. Now integration into a new community is necessary.

Reintegration into a faith community is an important first step. Chaplains can assist in finding this supportive community of the victim's choice. It must be one that will not judge the person by his past life and will be willing and able to help him maintain his new commitments. Both chaplains and VVOVs must realistically face the fact that many groups will not be open to this. With involvement in a helpful faith community, chaplains begin to the end the contract with the victim.

Victims frequently need help in finding a place to live that is conducive to his new life style. Relocation into the old neighborhood is not encouraged. Chaplains must constantly search for available programs and organizations to help with this need.

Other reintegrations may include relocation into the work force and a responsible family life. Now that a victim has learned to legally work for a living, it may be necessary that he learn how to save money for the future. Finally, he needs to be reintegrated into the community that has helped him. He has been helped and it is often helpful for him to give back to the society by helping others. Many VVOVs become very effective in working with this special population because of their experience. Knowing first hand the efforts involved in rehabilitation, they can become true wounded healers.

CONCLUSION

Working with this population requires lots of patience, diligence, carefulness, creativity, and technical professionalism; it can be a rough and difficult road. The hoped for outcomes, however, will minimize the weight. Recognizing the problem of violence as a contagious epidemic that can destroy us must energize us as professional chaplains. For society, investing in facilitating change for even a few VVOVs means saving millions of dollars that otherwise would be spent yearly to care for this patient population. More importantly, for society and the VVOVs themselves, it means precious valuable lives reintegrated into our human communities.

REFERENCES

Dykstra, Robert C. *Counseling Troubled Youth.* Louisville, KY: Westminster John Knox Press, 1997.

Peterson, Eugene H. *Five Smooth Stones of Pastoral Work.* Grand Rapids, Eerdmans Publishing Company, 1980.

The Dance with *The Discipline*

Kathy C. Spivey, DMin

SUMMARY. The author became acquainted with *The Discipline* only recently and this article describes two pastoral visits in which *The Discipline* provides guidance for interactive presence. Thus this material represents how the author seeks to grasp and integrate it into her clinical practice in a short time. *[Article copies available for a fee from The Haworth Document Delivery Service: 1-800-342-9678. E-mail address: <getinfo@haworth pressinc.com> Website: <http://www.HaworthPress.com> © 2001 by The Haworth Press, Inc. All rights reserved.]*

KEYWORDS. Psychiatric pastoral visits, chaplain, pastoral care, measurement, outcomes

Routine in one's work is a piece. I find ministry to be no exception in that regard as a hospital chaplain. Then, I believe, there is the challenge of staying mindful in the midst of one's particular landscape. Tools can be useful, supportive aids that foster imaginative, creative, insightful ways to enter into one's experience in the moment and reflectively.

I joined the Spiritual Care Services Staff at Barnes-Jewish Hospital (BJH) in June 1999 as Chaplain for Psychiatric Services (in-patient). Just prior to this transition, I served as Lead Chaplain in the Long Term Care setting within the same health care system for nearly two years. During this time, a colleague in the departmental CPE residency program shared a draft description of *The Discipline* and his enthusiasm for this mate-

The Reverend Kathy C. Spivey is Chaplain for Psychiatric Services, Barnes-Jewish Hospital, One Barnes-Jewish Hospital Plaza, St. Louis, MO 63110 (E-mail: KCS9988@ bjc.org).

rial spurred my interest. Amazingly, without a clear, in depth sense of its dimensions, I saw within its structure a way to fashion an "assessment tool" on paper for charting purposes for my Long Term Care setting. This I shared with Chaplain Lucas as an outcome of my initial wrestling with the document. So when I arrived as Psychiatric Staff Chaplain, our conversations continued to unfold as I presented assessment struggles in my new clinical area–Psychiatry.

Partly, I needed a stronger information base diagnostically in my clinical area, but Chaplain Lucas also kept speaking in this *foreign* language about "desired contributing outcomes." My language was about doing my ministry well, effectively. He assured me we were in the same ballpark. He challenged me to keep thinking about my contribution as a Spiritual Care Giver to the overall plan of care for our patients, as it meshed with other disciplines. How would I know when I was done for now?

He defined "desired contributing outcomes" this way–"what flows for the patient from what we are and do . . . the effect experienced by the patient." In the stir of getting to know the patient, in distilling needs, hopes and resources from their invited stories and sharing of experience, what do I hope for with him or her? What might we be able to work toward? What is my prayer for this patient?

Once I began to train myself more consciously to listen for and gently inquire about the patient's needs, hopes and resources, beyond simply listening in a broad way for themes of concern, I discovered I was gaining more information and insight to follow through in my care giving. My APIE (Assessment, Plan, Intervention(s), and Evaluation) process took on more flesh, so to speak. Let me briefly illustrate this awareness from two patient visits.

In the first situation, a psychiatric in-patient came to me on recommendation from her doctor in order to receive spiritual support. As a Day Hospital patient, this African American woman in her 40's had attended a Spirituality Group that I led and the discussion had sparked some new insights for her. She began to see her spirituality as a tool for her healing process and she requested a Chaplain's visit that her doctor affirmed with a written order. In our visit, the patient reminded me of our previous contact in the group setting and she relaxed into more conversation when I assured her that I remembered her, that I felt honored in her seeing me as a potential resource now. Over approximately forty minutes time, she insightfully shared her struggles with major depression and current life circumstances that led her to this hospitalization. She affirmed that her relationship with God was important, though she had felt recently depleted of energies to maintain some of her usual spiritual disciplines–reading Scripture, praying, attending worship. We discovered a mutual love for writing and her aspirations to one day publish the novels she sought to create. Socially, she acknowledged withdrawing more and more. This she knew was not a healthy posture.

Given her energies and marked enthusiasm about her writing, I invited her to consider getting on the mailing list of a local university "International Writers Center," exploring community college offerings for an evening class to support her writing interests, and/or seeking out a writer's group. These options would provide both social stimulation and more room to develop her writing interest. I further suggested journaling as a prayer tool, even if her prayers could only be a sentence or two, or maybe just a phrase or cluster of words from a Psalm reading each day. I encouraged her to begin searching for a church community, taking the next six months to explore several different congregations, beginning close to home. The spirit of *possibility* and *structure* in these suggestions held her interest. They felt "do-able" at her own pace. They felt like "healthy options" and she admitted to feeling "encouraged" about getting her life back on track. We then prayed for her healing and for the courage to take these next steps. She further expressed her gratitude for our time, acknowledging that her spirit felt "lighter."

My second illustration involves a Caucasian female in her early fifties, also suffering from major depression complicated by a significant grief issue–the suicide of her eldest child (an adult son) within the past eighteen months. A doctor's written orders prompted my referral visit. Following introductions in her room, we moved to a private interview space on her unit for further conversation. I invited her to share with me how she understood her current hospitalization. What might be weighing on her spirit? That was nearly all the nudging she needed. For the next two hours, I worked intently to listen to her story. Layers of loss were uncovered, woven through other deaths of close family members from her family of origin, through her marriage ending with strains of abuse, and then her son's suicide–a period of some thirty plus years of painful loss and memory. Gently, as I listened, I inquired how had she coped over time? Was there some pattern of information now that seemed clearer to her about what had sustained her to this point? Who had she looked to for help or support–friends, other family members, a professional counselor, a church community? What spiritual tools did she use (prayer, inspirational reading, walks in nature)? Was a relationship with the Holy a resource she felt connected to, and if so, in what way(s)?

As she talked, she began to see more clearly how she had modeled most of her grieving after the style used by her mother. Her mother had lost a son years ago, the patient's elder brother with whom the patient had a close relationship into early adulthood when he died suddenly of heart failure. After his funeral, her mother had gone to her bedroom and stayed for weeks. When she emerged, she rarely left home for months and there was little talk about the deceased. My patient began to recognize that her mother's solution was not practical or helpful to her. Though she had not shut herself off in walled rooms, the patient had enclosed her losses in a room of her heart without proper attending. I wondered out loud if part of her depression now was "breakdown to break through"? Perhaps, it was time to attend to that room of painful memories in order to free herself for "new life." She responded with acknowledging this held a ring of truth for her. She began to recount encouragement from her other two adult children to invest more in her self, her interests, even new relationships to meet her needs for adult friendship. There was more to life than being super grandma and a caring mother. She then began to share stories of tea parties she threw for her neighbors, deliberately inviting one person currently going through a difficult divorce from her husband of 30 plus years. How she missed her former antiques and crafts business that she had given up some few years ago. She had enjoyed the people connected with it. She also acknowledged some recent passing thoughts about going back to church, recalling teaching Sunday School to children in earlier years.

Finally, I must share that she was tearful through much of the last hour of our visit. How they flowed, not with deep sobs, but with a quiet steadiness that kept using up every tissue we had between us. She reflected, "You are the first person who has been willing to let me talk about all this, just talk. I've needed this." I felt affirmed although also weary from the pace we had kept for two hours. I asked her if she liked to read. "Yes," that she had even gotten away from that pleasurable activity. I offered to bring her some printed materials on grieving that she agreed would be helpful to her. I asked if we might close our time with prayer. She accepted willingly. I prayed in thanksgiving for the power of and insight from our stories, for the gift of tears, for the hope of new life, and the courage to give attention to her difficult memories. As we parted, and I went to chart, even in my weariness I could sense the movement, the shift that occurred for her. How meaningful is the dance of Spirit, discipline, and doing the moment faithfully.

As final comment, let me express how I experienced my chaplaincy as different resultant to my exposure to *The Discipline.* Rather than going into these situations with ears wide open, I went in with ears open and with movable antennae. My listening felt better directed as I concentrated on attending to and inquiring about the patients' "needs, hopes, and resources" as their stories unfolded. My inquiries were dedicated, focused toward a more specific way of gathering information so as to develop "a profile" of the patient. I moved beyond collecting scattered facts only to be overwhelmed by them, to being more poised to gather and then sift their information in search of a direction of care. Rather than feeling overwhelmed and asking myself, "Now what do I do?" I felt empowered to initiate suggestions or to ponder out loud noticing a meaningful connection. Did this ring true for them–this need, that hope, this resource or lack thereof? I sensed more agility in my work with the patients to help set a strategy for renewed self-care. My charting then also reflected my specific interventions and whether or not my spiritual assessment was complete for this admission or open to further follow up support to the patient. This held more weight of integrity to me as part of a multidisciplinary team, for spiritual care accountability. I say again, how meaningful the dance of Spirit, discipline and doing the moment faithfully.

First Steps:
Approaching *The Discipline* Based, Outcome Oriented Ministry Model

Elisha D. Donaldson, MDiv

SUMMARY. This article describes how a new staff chaplain is approaching and applying a discipline based, outcome oriented ministry model. He describes his move from being a lone, geriatric chaplain in a long term care facility to becoming a member of a team of staff chaplains in a teaching hospital who have disciplined themselves to an outcome oriented ministry model. The writer gives his perspective on *The Discipline,* and denotes ways in which his ministry has been impacted. Though the author has been involved with this process for only six months, both he and those in his care are experiencing some of the benefits of making tangible contributions and developing measurable outcomes in ministry

KEYWORDS. Chaplain, pastoral care, outcomes, neurology, discipline

Prior to joining the spiritual care team at Barnes-Jewish Hospital (BJH) I served as the staff chaplain at one of BJC Health System's long-term care/skilled nursing facilities. As compared to ministry in the hospital setting, providing spiritual care in the geriatric community was quite different. As with discipline based, outcome oriented minis-

Elisha D. Donaldson is Staff Chaplain, Neurology Services, Barnes-Jewish Hospital, One Barnes-Jewish Hospital Plaza, St. Louis, MO 63110 (E-mail: EDD8358@ BJC.org).

try, a spiritual assessment tool was utilized but not nearly to its fullest potential. As a clinician, I assessed patient's needs, hopes, and resources, determined what seemed to be the appropriate intervention(s), developed a plan for ministry and implemented that plan. Now as I reflect upon many of those ministry encounters, I realize that my assessments of their hopes and resources were sometimes limited by the context of the patient's realities. For instance, if a patient hoped they would go home, but, due to their medical condition or lack of resources, this hope could never be realized, I saw it as my responsibility to lead them toward a more realistic hope. In doing so, I had, for instance, labeled their hopes or lack of resources as a need to grieve or redefine meaning for their lives. If I had given more attention to outcomes and measurements by means of placing more importance on the ministry relationship, I would have given more attention to the hopes and resources of those patients. Based on my contact with *The Discipline,* I am convinced that chaplains cannot develop accurate outcomes and measurements without the inclusion and application of the patient's needs, hopes, and resources.

MY PERSPECTIVE

What I have learned thus far about discipline based, outcome oriented ministry is that the focus is not on what the caregiver does, but on the results of a pastoral relationship. The clinician then is more than just an individual with a skill, he or she is an artistic apprentice who has learned to respect, engage, and enhance the relationship for the best possible outcome. Therefore *The Discipline* allows the spiritual caregiver to become a manager of the relationship rather than an impotent dictator. A good manager will teach, guide, help, and encourage those he manages in hopes that by working together the goals can be achieved. A poor manager then, is one who simply bellows out repetitious dictates or who seeks to accomplish the objectives alone and feels that he/she solely bears the responsibility for the outcome. With discipline based, outcome oriented ministry, the results are ever evolving in synchronization with the subject(s) and the needs, hopes, and resources they bring.

APPROACHING THE DISCIPLINE: BECOMING AN APPRENTICE

What excites me most about outcome-oriented ministry is its methodology. Upon joining the staff, the first question I asked myself was,

"Where or how do I begin?" Somehow I knew the direction in which I was to embark, but I was very unsure of how big or small those first steps should be. Once I entered this environment I noted how each of the staff chaplains had developed significant diagnosis specific expertise in their clinical areas. While there may be many common themes among various patients and families facing various kinds of crisis, the resounding themes emanating from a stroke patient can have a different intonation from that of a patient with multiple sclerosis (MS). Working in long-term care I had become all too familiar with the common themes among the disabled geriatric residents. Now as the chaplain to neurology patients, I had to learn a new cadence in order to begin formulating accurate contributions, outcomes, and measurements. I quickly realized that the first step *The Discipline* mandated was that I become an apprentice. I use this term because the apprentice not only involves learning but also includes practicing instantaneously what is learned.

LEARNING THE NATURE OF THE ILLNESS

As an apprentice, my primary objectives are to become well educated about the nature of the illnesses, diseases, and conditions that bring patients to the Neurology Service. I have realized that there is a direct correlation between understanding the condition and developing accurate and measurable contributing outcomes. The greater challenge is not to gain knowledge about neurology patients in general, but to learn the specifics of the many diagnoses that define this medical specialty. I can recall my first week on the Neurological Intensive Care Unit when I was called to provide spiritual care to a family who's loved one was believed to be brain dead. I remember the anxiety I felt inside as I pondered over how, when, and what it would be like for me to be a part of the team that would approach this family about organ donation. Once I learned intrinsically what brain death was, I felt a sense of empowerment and peace. Repeatedly, families experiencing this crisis have expressed appreciation for the strength and consolation they have received through spiritual care that has enabled them to see/find meaning beyond their loss. If I had not obtained an in-depth understanding of brain death, that therapeutic transfer would not have occurred. In my care of families in this situation, a measurable outcome is to help them accept the reality of the death evidenced by expressions of grief and closure. One of my interventions toward this outcome is to help families understand brain death.

LEARNING HOW THE ILLNESS IMPACTS PATIENTS AND FAMILIES

My secondary objective as an apprentice is to gain insight into the ways in which patients and families are impacted by their disease, illness or condition. This objective requires the employment of active listening skills. It has been said that one must listen to the mundane in order to discover the pain. Since becoming a chaplain in neurology, I have become more intentional in my listening because I realize that if I fail in this area, I fail in all. I yet have to ignore the satisfaction that comes with discerning a patient's needs, which is self-empowering, and listen further to hear their hopes and resources, which empowers both patient and family. In learning the nature of the various diagnoses and the accompanying themes from patients and families I am able then to begin formulating precise contributing outcomes and measurements.

I have now had several ministry encounters with MS patients. One of the predominant themes I have heard is fear. Some focused on their fear of having another crisis or the fear of death. Using *The Discipline,* I have begun my preliminary development of appropriate contributing outcomes for MS patients. I know that as my database of experiences with these patients enlarges so my outcomes for this particular class of neurology patients will become more refined and accurate.

While working late one evening, I established a pastoral relationship with a 50-year-old male, post crisis, MS patient. He had lived with the disease for many years, and he was now relegated to living the rest of his life in a wheel chair. He was miserably alone for he had lived many decades estranged from his family and the God of his childhood. This crisis seemed to intensify his fears about dying and going to hell. As a result of employing *The Discipline* I was able not only to hear his needs, but also his hopes and resources and to formulate interventions toward appropriate, measurable outcomes. Yes, I was able to leave that ministry relationship feeling good because the patient felt good, but there was more; out of that ministry relationship this dying man determined to live out his death sentence by actively pursuing reconciliation with his family and his God. Now that's measurable!

GOOD OUTCOMES REQUIRE TIME

Since becoming a neurology chaplain, I have come to the realization that good outcomes require good ministry. What this means is that as a chaplain I must resist the urge to mimic the medical staff who make swift, mini visits in order to see more patients. As spiritual care givers we must have the same focus and discipline as Christ who declared that He would, "leave the fold of ninety-nine in order to save one that was lost." Listening takes time, and time is money, but a favorable outcome is worth the investment to attain it. As I reflect over my ministry in the geriatric community I can recall the pressures within and without to see every patient. This outcome-oriented discipline will not work effectively if quality is compromised for the sake of quantity.

But how can I spend the time needed in order to do a thorough assessment and follow through, and yet fulfill my responsibilities as a part of the care team? One afternoon while sitting in my weekly Stroke Management and Recovery Team (SMART) meeting, I received a revelation. As I listened to each of the various disciplines report their assessment of each patient I began thinking unrealistically, "We should have an accompanying spiritual assessment for every patient!" Then I became angry when I realized that I was the only one on the team who had patient care assignments on several different floors. Upon return to my reality and the reality of spiritual care in health care today, I began educating and prompting other team members on how to identify and make referrals for spiritual care. Teaching health care partners to identify those patients who need immediate spiritual intervention only affirms the chaplain's role as a specialist.

I have discovered that utilizing staff to identify urgent spiritual needs is dually beneficial, (1) it affirms the spirituality of the other team members and (2) it enlarges, extends, and helps to maintain the quality of spiritual care.

As stated above, employing this outcome-oriented discipline will demonstrate the value of spiritual care. Given the shortage of health care dollars and the intense scrutiny of everyone, spiritual care givers must have something more than a mere certificate of ordination or clerical ornaments. We must prove our worth through measurable outcomes. So what does it mean to prove our worth through *measurable* outcomes? It means that we make *tangible* contributions to the improvement of the lives of the patient's and families in our care. It means that we have employed an instrument, that when skillfully applied, provides empowerment for spiritual growth and healing. This outcome-oriented discipline has this potential and more.

Playing Well with Others:
The Discipline in a Pediatric Hospital

Leslie Weinstein, MA

SUMMARY. This article contains a personal reflection on the way it feels, in fact and in theory, to move from a chaplaincy position in a clinical setting, to one where clinical chaplaincy is relatively new. The article presents the ways a clinically trained chaplain can introduce herself to a new setting, and how she must continually reevaluate her approach.

KEYWORDS. Chaplain, pastoral care, spiritual assessment

Going from an urban, adult acute care hospital to a children's hospital has been a little like homesteading, though the admonition to "go west" would have to be revised to "go north a couple of blocks." Despite the closeness in distance, the hospitals were worlds apart in what their staffs and patients expected from chaplaincy. So, in the tradition of my forefathers, I staked my claim at my new workplace and set about the business of chaplaincy.

My training and initial experience at a large, acute care hospital in clinical chaplaincy suited me perfectly. The focus was, and remains, to be open and present to each patient according to his or her clinical diagnosis, with heightened regard for the resulting impact upon that

Chaplain Leslie Weinstein is affiliated with the St. Louis Children's Hospital, 1 Children's Place, St. Louis, MO 63110.

individual's spiritual life. Heart patients, for example, face issues different from those faced by liver transplant or oncology patients. The prevailing question for me as chaplain was, then, how does a patient's spirituality or religious beliefs help him or her cope, and give him or her hope in the future, while dealing with a particular illness? Further, what are the outcomes of my interactions and how do they impact the patient's healing? I loved learning how to be present for patients, helping them explore their spiritual selves.

When I heard about the opening at the nearby children's hospital, I felt it was for me. The hospital's first choice for the job had declined at the last minute, and I was able to step in. The interviewing and hiring experience was not unlike the way I got into Clinical Pastoral Education at the start. I simply went with the flow of it, feeling it was right. I was hired as their second chaplain, and my friend, the original chaplain, had been there for 20 years. He had been stretched so thin you could practically hear his bones snapping on a busy day. My being there would allow him to devote his time to the intensive care unit, trauma team and transplant teams which were demanding more and more of him. So my coming onto the scene, even as a part-time person, represented a big change for the users and providers of spiritual care.

The things I had been trained to do–spiritual assessments, attending multi-disciplinary meetings, rounds, charting–were new to my new environment. But these were skills which had become automatic to me, and the original chaplain encouraged me to bring this disciplined approach with me to the pediatric setting. As an optimist, I tend to believe that if I do my job well, people will like it, even if it's different from what they expect. So I forged ahead. My clinical areas included oncology/hematology, bone marrow transplant, neurology/neurosurgery and rehab. The staffs on these services were not used to seeing a chaplain nearly every day, much less one who charted, attended medical rounds, gathered data using a spiritual assessment tool and expected to be a fully responsible member of the health care team.

Sometimes they smiled at me, but mostly they looked at me as if to say, "You seem pleasant enough, but get away from me, I'm busy."

I couldn't believe they wouldn't welcome a clinical chaplain to the team, so I looked first for easy answers. Maybe it was because I'm a woman, or Jewish, or part-time. However, my optimism kicked back in. Rejecting sexism, flat out, has always served me well, so why stop now? The fact that I'm Jewish was a little harder to handle, though I view Judaism as my personal faith and not my mission as a chaplain. I consider myself a clinical chaplain serving a multi-faith community.

For me, being clinical means learning as much as I can about the illnesses that strike my patients, and studying how those illnesses tend to impact them and their families. Serving in a multi-faith environment allows me to draw upon both my life experiences and my religious studies background to assist others in using their spirituality as a resource for coping, hoping and imagining the future. The beauty of CPE for me was learning how to use and value my life experience while checking it at the door of each patient's room. My only agenda is how I can be present for patients, family and staff, helping them to reflect on the spiritual strength they possess within themselves, for themselves? This is a far cry from denominational chaplaincy. Even with my bedside prayers and rituals, I try to "speak in the language of the recipient," on behalf of him or her, to his or her vision of the Holy. Language, in fact, is how I view spirituality and religion. We each discover a way of expressing ourselves to G-d or nature or the universe, and that can equal religion, but it surely equals spirituality. When we cry out, "Why me," we want someone or something to hear us. I hope to be the conduit for that message, the one who puts it into the correct in-box, so to speak.

In new situations, people make assumptions. I assumed I could rush in with my method of chaplaincy and be accepted. The reason I received blank looks had less to do with me than with the overwhelming schedule everyone keeps. Another person (me) could equal more work for them, so I needed to prove myself in the field. And I have to point out here that effective clinical chaplaincy works best when it's supported by staff–lack of support can undermine a chaplain's ability to fully do the job. So I had to step back and take a look at myself.

One of the results of my life and work experience is a tendency to ignore office politics. My attitude is a result of being present at many more deaths than I can remember. I've been left with the feeling that we all generally engage in too much nonsense and I just don't want to play. High school was a long time ago, after all. However, not everyone copes like I do. By rejecting the idea that hospital politics matter, I was also rejecting one way that people cope. So in stepping back, I realized I needed to establish trust with others, learn about the staff, hospital and patients and allow them to learn about me. After all, my way of doing chaplaincy was great for me at an adult facility, but it needs tailoring for a children's hospital.

So many of the spiritual issues relevant to adult patients are turned upside down in pediatrics. Adult patients usually speak for themselves, either directly or through advance directives, while children rarely do. For adults, quality of life is often the number one issue, while with children, parents see quantity of life as paramount. Adults usually suffer in silence when they receive an injection, but kids can't always do that, so we as care givers must get accustomed to hearing screaming and crying in the halls. On the other hand, in situations such as chemotherapy, when adults can be most verbal, children keep quiet. Further, I haven't met one child or teenager yet who knew what a chaplain is, so they have no pre-conceived notions about us. They rarely have any ideas about church, G-d or religion, either. Even when they attend religious services weekly, younger kids don't think through why. It's something they do with their parent(s). Yet, children are profoundly spiritual beings. They walk with G-d and take it for granted.

I've been at my new position a little over six months. The people on my floors know who I am, and employees on the elevators and in the cafeteria are beginning to recognize me. I'm using a fairly simple spiritual assessment tool with patients and families, and will develop it as time goes on. Nearly every week I do an inservice program either on religious diversity or death and dying. And yet, a doctor recently told me that, while I'm welcome to come to his team meetings, he "doesn't consider chaplains part of the medical team, because patients and families should feel safe talking with the chaplain." Although disturbed by this old-fashioned opinion, I took it as a challenge. Here's a man who needs education about clinical chaplaincy. And, knowing that he has no time or patience for lectures from me, it's best if I make myself known with patients and their families, and in our team meetings. I will keep doing what I'm doing, and maybe he will change his view over time.

Last week I spent time with a very sick ten-year-old girl who told me that G-d is "the wind" to her. In that moment, everything else fell away and I was left with this knowledge: I'm in a blessed place where everyone works to heal children, and I will find my place here. Forging into this new territory reminds me daily of the odd twists and turns life offers. We can't look into the eyes of a suffering child and remark, "all things happen for a reason," because it's simply not true. As witnesses to this suffering, we as nurses, doctors, social workers and chaplains must constantly weigh not only what we're doing but also how we're doing it. I can only be responsible for myself and I am very hopeful about the future. The adventure is truly just beginning.

RELATIONSHIPS OF THE DISCIPLINE TO CLINICAL PASTORAL EDUCATION AND OTHER AREAS OF MINISTRY

Experience with Clinical Pastoral Education in the Context of *The Discipline*

Arthur M. Lucas, MDiv, BCC

SUMMARY. This article relates the experience of integrating *The Discipline* into the process and curriculum of an ACPE accredited clinical pastoral education (CPE) program involving residents and single unit students. It describes supervisor and student concerns as well as the conclusions they reached concerning the integration of *The Discipline* into The CPE process.

KEYWORDS. Chaplain, pastoral care, clinical pastoral education, CPE, outcomes

The Reverand Arthur M. Lucas is Director, The Department of Spiritual Care Services, Barnes-Jewish Hospital at Washington University Medical Center, One Barnes-Jewish Plaza, St. Louis, MO 63110 (E-mail: AML2792@bjc.org).

As described in a previous article in this publication, the chaplains of Barnes-Jewish Hospital (BJH) have developed a model for providing pastoral care that is discipline based and outcome oriented. *The Discipline* is based on a careful, replicable spiritual assessment, planning and evaluation process. The process involves assessment of patient needs, hopes and resources that results in a spiritual profile. Given the spiritual profile, desired contributing outcomes are identified with the patient that will contribute to healing and well-being. A plan for facilitating those contributions is formed, the planned interventions given, and the contributing outcomes evaluated in light of the intended contributions. While technical in structure, the process of *The Discipline* is largely content free. Chaplains must remain attuned, even dependent, on the patient for its substance, desired contributing outcomes, plan, and interventions. The model is implemented as a dynamic process open to the heart, story, and person of the patient. *The Discipline* requires the chaplain to be consistently available and intentional.

We built this approach on the assumption that patients and families need to be better off because of a chaplaincy presence, better off than if chaplains were not present. Chaplains make their visits to make a difference, a difference for the good of the other (patient, family, staff person, physician, community) in circumstances that are naturally difficult. The difference that chaplains intend to make, however, must always be faithful to the values, the belief system, of those receiving care.

This assumption increased the stakes for our accountability, responsibility, intentionality, and authority. If our caring presence is good, how is it good? (The questions of interpersonal and intrapersonal dynamics). Toward what is that "good" directed? (The questions of intention and effect). How do we know? (The questions of observability and measurability). So What? (The questions of added value and contribution to care).

The department includes an Association for Clinical Pastoral Education accredited clinical pastoral education program, including a full year residency, summer internships, and part-time externships. The CPE programs are an integral part of the department and service. We have always seen our trainees as adult, professional caregivers and learners. They are first of all here to make a difference for the good of our patients, families and staff. Supervisory responsibility includes making clinical assignments that require the level of skill, integration, and continuity that is possible for them and in which they can mature as care givers.

As *The Discipline* became the model for the department's chaplaincy, we became aware that we needed to integrate it into our CPE program. This was both an interest and a concern to the department director and another CPE supervisor. The supervisor found himself saying some things to CPE students that were inconsistent with departmental clinical practices. He oriented CPE students to a simple, comparatively unilateral emphasis on being present, personally available, and self-aware during care giving. At the same time, the staff chaplains were being orienting toward being more intentional in and accountable for the differences we wish to make with *The Discipline*. The contrast was stark for the supervisor. The incongruity required attention.

The staff chaplains, having played significant roles in the development of *The Discipline,* naturally engaged the residents and interns with this approach although the CPE students were not hearing about it in their curriculum. In their clinical assignments, the students encountered a hospital culture that expected and reinforced many of the basic values and assumptions of *The Discipline.* Given the contextual nature of the CPE process, it was necessary to correct this incongruity.

The first attempt at integrating *The Discipline* into the CPE model took place in a 1995-96 Extended Unit supervised by the author and Robert Yim, a Supervisor-In-Training. Chaplain Yim had been an integral participant in developing *The Discipline* and our intent was to focus on heart care (with coronary artery bypass graft patients, heart transplant patients, heart surgery patients), thoracic care (with lung transplant patients, volume reduction surgery patients, cystic fibrosis patients) and oncology care (with bone marrow transplant patients, chemotherapy patients). We also intended to consciously integrate *The Discipline's* format and structure in our supervision of these students.

Based on what we most valued in the action/reflection model for learning, our concerns included:

1. Creating cookie cutter pastoral care givers by truncating the struggle and search inherent to the CPE process by giving "the" way to give care; turning action/reflection into see/do. But, we knew our chaplains were not clones even after developing and owning *The Discipline,* and so we reassured ourselves that each student still shaped and brought texture to their ministry.

2. Blunting students' search and discovery process for their own pastoral identity and way of developing that identity. But we knew the staff chaplains were still struggling as they continued to develop in their calling and profession. We trusted this would also be true for students.
3. Reinforcing (many) student's tendency to "do" rather than "be with" or "journey" with patients; subjugating presence and awareness to role and function. But, we knew from experience that adopting a more disciplined way of providing pastoral care actually enhanced the focus and intensity of the journey.
4. Reverting the Supervisor-Group-Process-Integration model to a teacher-classroom-didactic-acquisition model. As supervisors, however, we believed that how we modeled this more disciplined, outcome orientation would minimize this difficulty.
5. Subjugating the heart/gut of caring to the head/thought. We knew from our experience the demands of *The Discipline* passively invited more "head work" but we also had learned it tended to intensify the demand we attend to feelings.
6. Projecting an importance of certainty over risk. Our experience had taught us that, when *done well*, *The Discipline* allowed plenty of room for surprises, and in fact sharpened our ability to notice them.

We consciously implemented the teaching of *The Discipline* during orientation, before they were seeing patients. We taught it as the care model developed by our chaplains and effective in our clinical setting. We included introductions to the chaplaincy of the staff chaplains in their clinical specialty areas. Each staff chaplain described the spiritual dynamics in his/her area and the contributing outcomes s/he commonly intended as a spiritual caregiver with patients/families in that area. We integrated aspects of *The Discipline* into the verbatim format including segments on spiritual assessment, spiritual care planning, and evaluation of care. We explicitly used the basic questions within *The Discipline* in individual and group supervision and exploring each student's work with his/her patients and families.

As supervisors, we discussed the group and individual supervision sessions and reflected on how consistent we were being in integrating and leveraging the milieu of our hospital and department for the students' training. Because the supervisor-in-training was just beginning his supervisory work, there were frequent opportunities to discuss the process in terms of fresh, concrete examples, specific supervisory dynamics, and theories. These discussions also gave the senior supervisor ample opportunity to consider how this unit was different from usual past units he had supervised.

As the extended unit proceeded we were pleased with the group process. The Externs were able to form a group and to engage more substantive and often confrontive material. We were pleased with the personally unique ways they engaged *The Discipline* and were using it with patients. They were searching and struggling with their pastoral identity and authority. In our perception, the searching process so common in CPE began more quickly and became more intense than previously observed. Feedback about their ministry was positive from the patient care areas.

Similar changes were made in two ensuing summer units and another extended unit. After each unit, we sought feedback without any specific indications of special concerns. The feedback included:

1. The basic, common language about spiritual care provided by *The Discipline* facilitated reflection and group building.
2. The necessity and freedom to develop themselves as pastoral care givers was at times overwhelming. Experiencing the necessity to develop themselves as pastoral care givers came through focusing on the effect of their care for the healing and well-being of patients. Simultaneously, they experienced active support that encouraged them to develop their own unique pastoral identity and theology. The combination was intense, personal, and right in front of them most of the time.
3. They experienced stress in their effort to discover, identify and develop their own pastoral identity and way of caring. They were heartened by the awareness that their current and future ministry makes a real difference for people in their care.
4. They experienced supervisory input to their learning process as less than they wished. They were hungry for more input to inform their ministry and development.
5. They affirmed the uniqueness of the program and supervisory engagement for their learning and growth as individuals and as a peer group.
6. They found that *The Discipline* gave purpose to spiritual assessment because it provided a context of caring and feeding the care giving process.

7. They found *The Discipline,* taken as a whole, to be overwhelming. They just could not think about all of it at once. Approached as a whole, all at once, it was often intimidating, and too technical.

We understood this feedback to mean that teaching *The Discipline* was compatible with the core CPE values. In fact, for some, teaching the discipline-based model enhanced the process by providing a common language and base for beginning pastoral care givers.

The model described above was rather intensely front-end loaded with input during orientation. We began to test the effects of providing information and pastoral care models during orientation. This seemed to decrease what seemed to us as unnecessary anxieties for the learning process. Anxiety about how or where to even start, how to begin to understand what they heard and saw and felt, and how all this mattered in the first place suddenly became less necessary for the student's learning. With the infusion of front-end input those trainee anxieties refocused to anxiety about the human, theological complexities of good pastoral care giving. The urgency within the trainees to find their own identity relative to the model and in their relationships with patients, families and each other was at least as intense as that of students in previous quarters.

We have now integrated *The Discipline* into our residency program, a part of the St. Louis Cluster, ACPE residency. We begin with an eight day, heavily didactic orientation process, covering material including (a) health care ethics and consultation, (b) grief and grief ministry, (c) requesting tissue and organ donation in a context of grief care, (d) major religious traditions and health care, (e) providing pastoral care with people of other cultures and ethnicity than our own, (f) differences between a social and a pastoral visit, (g) basics in hospital visitation, (h) active listening skills, (i) coping, (j) staff care and relating to the employee assistance program and (k) charting, along with the previously described training in *The Discipline* in the specific clinical mentioned above.

We now have sufficient experience and student feed back to reflect carefully on the changes in our ACPE CPE curriculum. We believe that introducing *The Discipline* is best done in different ways in different contexts. At Barnes-Jewish Hospital, the milieu immediately and clearly supports a style of ministry that can be clear about what we know, how we know what we know, what that implies for care, what good is intended from our care, and what our care involves. The environment is crisp, professional, pointed, and fast moving. At another community hospital of 120 beds in one of the western suburbs of St. Louis, the environment is more informal, even in professional exchanges. There, we learned to introduce *The Discipline* minimally in orientation, then to integrate it into group and individual processes over time during the training process. When we introduced it as described above with intense didactic attention, the style was not supported because it led to more confusion than reflection.

We have learned that *The Discipline* is very abstract for students until they have sufficient clinical experience. We have slowed the introduction to extended unit students although we present the model more directly than at the community hospital described above. The elements are more thoroughly introduced and more explicitly a part of group and individual supervisory processes from the beginning. Less teaching on the front end with extended unit students and interns gives more time to accumulate experience needed to provide a context for reflection.

How *The Discipline* is introduced seems dependent on the professional, relational, and clinical milieu for the training. Students need a critical mass of clinical experience with patients, families, and staff to make the best use of it. The clinical experience pushes the model into the reality of their ministry.

We have also made additional adjustments that balance the heavy front-end load. For instance, the author had used a very concrete, formal learning contract that includes specific roles for the supervisor and the group, complete with indices and final measures. [Two or three supervisory hours were often needed to create the complete agreement.] He now uses a more covenantal approach to establishing a learning contract with students and a common understanding for the student's learning can be created within an hour's supervision time. This seems to provide balance and model a way of being pastorally disciplined and outcome oriented. Establishing learning goals and expectations in this way directly relates to the outcome orientation imbedded in *The Discipline* itself and in the departmental milieu. This covenantal rather than contractual modeling provides its own experience of the outcome orientation that is more relational and often more comfortable for students. The experience helps convey the humanness of a disciplined model for care giving and thereby counter balances the technical image of helping.

As *The Discipline* has become more generalized and expected throughout the hospital, we have kept close watch on the rising expectations of chaplains, including residents, interns, and extended-unit students. The expectations concerning consistency, integration, skill, and contribution continue to rise. This has made placement of residents within clinical areas increasingly difficult. Our intention is to place students in clinical areas where they can begin meeting needs and expectations from the beginning while being challenged to grow. We have, for example, found it increasingly difficult to place a first year resident in an area where staff expectations of chaplaincy match up well with the average resident. Since interns and part time students are assigned to specific patient subgroups within the clinical areas of staff chaplains, we are more easily able to make those service/learning matches effectively.

In summary, our reflections indicate these changes in the curriculum have:

1. Increased the ease for students and staff chaplains to engage each other.
2. Contributed to earlier student engagement of hospital staff and physicians.
3. Enabled student issues to emerge in and through the learning process. For instance one part-time student began using *The Discipline* more as a check-list of questions for patients, just the way his hyper structure and dependence on authority would have led him to do in any model of caring or supervising.
4. Provided a clearer, cleaner connection for the intra-personal work demanded for this ministry. The reason for attending to the student's intra-personal dynamics is more immediately connected with his/her interpersonal relationships and ministry experiences, much like *The Discipline* makes sense of assessment by putting it immediately in the context of care giving.
5. Increased accountability.
6. Heightened demand for students' creativity and flexibility.
7. Increased resilience. This is aided by having a model readily available that facilitates the student's ability to think through what might be missing or dysfunctional in what s/he offered a specific patient or has to offer in ministry.
8. Intensified anxieties about owning authority and accountability for care. The focus of this is often in identifying and owning the worth of their uniquely spiritual care profile and desired contributing outcomes. The dynamic is still imbedded in issues of authority and accountability.

9. Driven earlier attention to the complexities of the patient/family processes.
10. Made projections and over-identifications easier to confront, consistently asking the "How do you know?" question.

A last observation comes from a portion of the residency curriculum. During the Spring (third) Quarter of the last two years this author, as the St. Louis Cluster Supervisor responsible for the group structures, has facilitated a curriculum focusing on spiritual assessment. The reading and discussion introduces spiritual assessment models from Paul Pruyser (*The Minister as Diagnostician*), James Lapsley (*Salvation and Health*), Carol Gilligan (*In a Different Voice*), George Fitchett (7 by 7 Model), and nursing (presented by Valery Yancey, R.N., Ph.D.) as well as *The Discipline*. Discussions intend to work not only with the material presented, but also to facilitate resident awareness of the spiritual assessment model he/she was already using, usually preconsciously. Each resident then presents his/her own spiritual assessment model, along with a case that demonstrates its use. The residents with exposure to *The Discipline* were more likely to present a model integrating aspects of different models from the material in their own assessment methods. The residents from the other sites were more likely to adopt one of the presented models rejecting each of the others.

CONCLUSIONS

We have described how we introduced a discipline-based, outcome-oriented model for pastoral care into the curriculum. We have learned that the education process can thrive in a disciplined, outcome-oriented milieu that simultaneously emphasizes the person and presence of the caregiver with intentionality and accountability found in *The Discipline*. Early introduction of material that equips the students for giving attention to their "difference making" enhances the learning process as well as the care giving processes. As one supervisor said, "the process is alive and well and we can't kill it." Responsible introduction of didactic material that introduces *The Discipline* into the CPE action/reflection model can enhance both service and learning. We all seem a little less afraid of what we know and of teaching it.

The Discipline for Doing Spiritual Care: Variations on a Theme

James D. Daugherty, ThD, BCC

SUMMARY. This article describes the writer's introduction to *The Discipline* and his decision to utilize selected aspects of it in direct care and in an educational milieu. The first section describes adaptation of the Profile (Concepts of Holy, Meaning, Hope, and Community) in the writer's work with addicted persons on a Recovery Center. The second section presents the employment of this Profile as a way to introduce CPE interns to the art of pastoral assessment.

KEYWORDS. Chaplain, pastoral care, clinical pastoral education

INTRODUCTION

I was first introduced to *The Discipline* in the form presented in Art Lucas' article at an educational retreat for chaplains in the BJC Health System. Through prior experience with the author and other members of his spiritual services staff, I had already become acquainted with individual aspects of *The Discipline* and had incorporated them in my work as chaplain and CPE supervisor. Based on differences between

---

James D. Daugherty is affiliated with the Department of Pastoral Care, Christian Hospital Northeast-Northwest, 11133 Dunn Road, St. Louis, MO 63136 (E-mail: JDD7835@bjc.org).

our respective hospitals and chaplaincy staff, I chose not to utilize the fully developed Discipline as a tool for assessment throughout our department.

In addition to their value as tools for assessment, the selected features cited above proved to be valuable resources for the practice of ministry, or as vehicles for treatment, as it were. This was specifically the case with the area described in *The Discipline* as *Profile* with its categories of *Concept of Holy, Meaning, Hope,* and *Community.* These proved fruitful avenues for engaging the spirituality of patients in the Recovery Center where I led a spirituality group for persons dealing with alcohol and drug addiction.

The Discipline also provided resource material for the curriculum for our program in clinical pastoral education. Of primary value here were the elements *Needs/Hopes/Resources* and *Profile* (*Concept of Holy, Meaning, Hope, and Community*). In the material that follows, I describe how I used *The Discipline* in an abbreviated form to inform both ministry/treatment and education areas.

MINISTRY ON A RECOVERY CENTER

All treatment programs with which I am familiar stress the importance of relationship with a higher power if recovery is to be effective. They tend to assume that those attempting recovery understand the meaning of power and so will focus more consistently on the meaning and impact of the qualifying term "higher." Not so implicit is the understanding that "higher power" essentially refers to God "as we understand Him" (*sic.*).

Although I am in basic agreement with the thrust of this classic approach to recovery, two decades of experience in leading a spirituality group on our hospital's Recovery Center have taught me that if I were to help persons in recovery to "engage their spirituality," as *The Discipline* suggests, I would need to make some adjustments to the received tradition.

First, I reminded myself, consonant with *The Discipline,* that all persons possessed some form of spirituality and that my task was to engage that spirituality and not to attempt to inculcate my own.

Next, I discovered that the assumption that staff and persons in treatment generally understood the meaning of power in the same way was not at all the case. It became clear, therefore, that before addressing the meaning of God I needed to address the issue of power.

From Howard Clinebell, I gleaned the insight that persons addicted to alcohol are often seeking "God in a bottle." While attempting a spiritual journey, they are following a dead end path. My strategy was to tap into that basic instinct toward wholeness but to describe and to offer a different and challenging direction for their efforts. I could only offer a redemptive possibility; the decision for recovery was of course theirs.

My challenge was to describe the redemptive potential of recovery in terms that were understandable and that would engage addicted persons in their concrete, particular lives. It was at this point that an element of *The Discipline* provided a pathway into their lives and a means of countering resistance. This was the *Profile,* with its *Concept of Holy, Meaning, Hope* and *Community.* First of all, I presented to the group the view that we have been created to exercise power and then defined power as the capacity to influence one's environment. I then suggested that we influenced our environment as we struggled with meaning, hope, and community and that in the midst of the struggle one may come up against the Holy or God.

The overall thrust of my approach was to demonstrate that redemptive recovery required recognition of the distorted understanding of power that drives us toward violence, misunderstanding, and isolation and to encourage a movement toward changed understanding and behavior. A process that embodies awareness, acceptance, and forgiveness abetted the movement.

After some experience in employment of these elements of *The Discipline,* I changed the order of the elements, moving the *Concept of Holy* from first to fourth place in the order of reference. Addressing it at the outset often led either to overt resistance or to equally unhelpful pious responses. By structuring conversation around *Meaning, Hope, Community,* the *Concept of Holy* arose in more authentic and organic ways. Further there was a freedom not to talk directly about God at all but instead to work at identifying foundational structures of value, which for many was their God-equivalent.

A focus on *Meaning* helped group members to identify residual sources of meaning, such as family and job, and to vent feelings of meaninglessness relative to empty lives occasioned by addiction. By looking at *Hope,* they were often able to own the hopelessness of lives centered on drug use and also to begin to experience the rebirth of hope that often accompanies serious 12-step work. Perhaps most importantly, our stress on *Community,* on viewing redemptive recovery as a corporate event, served to facilitate their letting go of relationships that fostered addictive behavior rather than recovery. They were now beginning to affirm membership in a new community of seekers after wholeness.

Use of the *Profile,* with its four constitutive elements, served in the setting of this Recovery Center as a means to expose addicted persons to a view of human empowerment in which spiritual growth connects directly to recognizable areas of human engagement. Although the *Profile* did serve as an assessment tool, in this setting it functioned primarily as a structure for ministry or treatment.

CLINICAL PASTORAL EDUCATION

As noted above in the "Introduction," I was first introduced to *The Discipline* at an educational retreat for chaplains. Subsequent to this, and after conversation with Art Lucas, I decided to include *The Discipline* in the curriculum for my clinical pastoral education program.

The Discipline presented a thorough approach to doing spiritual care and challenged even experienced staff chaplains to employ it effectively. Such employment was almost always beyond the competency levels demonstrated by students in Introductory CPE. In light of this recognition, I decided to introduce *The Discipline* in its entirety to the CPE interns in our 1999 summer unit. It was my expectation that this would serve as an introduction to a method that required both assessment and intervention. It was my intent to re-visit *The Discipline* occasionally during the unit and to raise relevant aspects during our clinical work. On an ongoing and regular basis, I employed two of its elements to guide our critical reflection of pastoral work presented by the students. It was my hope that a limited use of *The Discipline* would both allay student anxiety and increase the quality of student critique; and in this I was not disappointed.

I chose as analytical elements two features of *The Discipline*: *Needs, Hopes and Resources;* and the *Profile* (*Concept of Holy, Meaning, Hope,* and *Community*). In the verbatim format that students used to present their pastoral work, I required an introduction/background of the patient, a pastoral plan, a verbatim account of the pastoral contact, and psychological, sociological, and theological assessments. Use of the elements from *The Discipline* worked well to help the students to flesh out their understanding of patients and their dynamic issues and to delve with increased critical acumen into pastoral concerns.

At first the students felt insecure in trying to utilize a method that was both new and daunting in its scope. They struggled to find ways to engage the "living human document" confronting them. They needed cues or clues that would assist them in going deeper. At this juncture, the Windows/Themes/Keys that provide avenues into the Needs/ Hopes and Resources of persons in crisis proved to be valuable resources, again for allaying student anxiety and for suggesting the myriad dimensions of human engagement.

Interestingly, in their use of the *Profile* in patient care, the students' experience was similar to mine with persons in recovery: namely, that they learned more about a patient's authentic or existential form of spirituality by exploring *Meaning, Hope,* and *Community* than by a frontal focus on the *Concept of Holy.* They were able, accordingly, to find God-talk in unexpected places. Expressed differently, person-centered talk and God-talk existed not as strict dichotomies but as elements in dialogue that both suggest and require the other.

By the end of the summer unit, these CPE interns had made clear strides in forging assessment tools that yielded increasingly more effective ministry to those whom they served. Assessment vocabulary had become more nearly their own; and they required little urging from me to employ it. Their success here was aided in no small measure, I believe, by use of selected features of *The Discipline.*

CONCLUSION

In the above discussion, I have attempted to demonstrate the appropriateness and the efficacy of utilizing selected elements from *The Discipline* for purposes of assessment, education, and direct care. Even though such adaptation and abbreviation clearly fail to do justice to the fullness of the schema, yet its originators would, I believe, find it an interesting and faithful expression of the intent of their efforts.

An Adaptation of *The Discipline* in a Clinical Pastoral Education Program

Larry Shostrom, PhD

SUMMARY. The author describes his perspective on providing pastoral care to hospital patients, his search for new ways to understand that ministry, his first contact with *The Discipline*, and his adaptation of it to the clinical and educational programs at his center. He discusses the need to help clinical pastoral education students to operationalize their ministry and to learn how to identify outcomes that are meaningful to health care decision makers.

KEYWORDS. Chaplain, pastoral care, outcomes, clinical pastoral education

Editor: To begin, would you describe how you learned about *The Discipline*?

LS: I first learned about it in 1997 when Art Lucas and I coincidentally had dinner together at a Herbert Benson Spirituality and

Larry Shostrom is Chaplain and Director, Department of Pastoral Care, University of Iowa Medical Center, Iowa City, IA (E-mail: shostrom@uiowa.edu).

This is an edited telephone interview between Dr. Shostrom and Larry Vande-Creek.

Health Conference in Los Angeles. Later he described *The Discipline* in a presentation to a regional meeting of the Association for Clinical Pastoral Education. I was already entertaining the idea of visiting the Department and seeing it in action; after that conference I made arrangements. A CPE student and I visited the Department for two days in February 1999.

Editor: So you took a CPE student with you?

LS: Yes, I took a second year student who provided pastoral care to palliative care patients. Since then I have made my own adaptation of it here. And I'm still working on adapting it, going back to my material once in a while and seeing how things fit. *The Discipline* provides a clear process and that intrigues me.

Editor: Can you describe that?

LS: Well, I have taught pastoral care for a long time now in the same way I learned it under supervision. That was a process of learning to emotionally be with patients and letting them identify issues. I experienced it as sort of like stumbling into something that's important. When the patient said something that sounded important, I would say, at least to myself, "Now I can help you with that issue." And then we would talk about the patient's concern. I have now provided ministry in two university research centers and I have become increasingly uncomfortable with the quality of pastoral care based on that older model. My discomfort was stimulated by nursing colleagues who have struggled with demands that they produce measurable clinical outcomes as well as by others who talk about the discipline of care plans. And then I would say to myself with increasing discomfort, "Well, what do we have in pastoral care that is complementary to such deliberate approaches?" I believe that we were doing good work when we used the old model and we were helpful to patients, but I felt increasingly that I was out of the dialog loop because we didn't go about our ministry in a parallel way. It's not that I wanted something identical to these other professions, but I felt that our clinical methodology was becoming increasingly outdated. As I began to struggle with this, I went back to some of Pruyser's and

McSherry's work about making spiritual assessments. Fitchett too has struggled with how we can pull consistent human themes out of patient stories, themes that link all humanity, even though people are individuals. Then I would talk with nurses about what they as a profession were trying to do with their own taxonomy of nursing. Clearly, it was helping them become more articulate about how nursing contributed to patient outcomes, differentiating their day-to-day work from just fulfilling the mandates and edicts of physicians. It was clear that they were taking a leadership role by constructing a parallel process that demonstrated their contribution to healing. And I feel that we have an active role in the healing process parallel with nursing and medicine. In that way we are different from social work, although we are frequently compared to them. When I talked with Chaplain Lucas I realized that he was putting words to my struggle, and that, although I was headed in the same direction, he was miles ahead of me. So, I said to myself, "Why reinvent the wheel? Let's see what he and his people have done and see how it adapts to my setting."

Editor: So, from your point of view *The Discipline* is about a structure, a point of view.

LS: Let me illustrate by describing what Kübler-Ross did when she began to study the dying process. She didn't set a structure. She put some labels on thematic processes and that's how I experienced *The Discipline*. The St. Louis team has critically examined and identified the spiritual themes that people experience. They have also looked at the process of pastoral care and described that process. They put some labels on it and described it. So they didn't really invent something. What they've done is taken something that we've done and refined it. I don't think they've invented care maps. What they've done is begun to categorize material that they've collected from the stories of their patients. One of the things I remember from my conversation in St. Louis was–although this is not an exact quote–

> After we've talked to 100 patients, we don't have to listen to all the stories of patient 101 because what that person is going to say is likely nothing really new. It's

likely to be some variation on what many of the 100 patients talked about. So we have some sort of expectation of what the person is going to say, what the person needs, and how to focus the conversation.

And that's what *The Discipline* is about. The clinical process uses the Chaplain's memory of people's stories and they've identified themes out of that data bank.

Editor: So chaplains have these themes in their heads and, after the individual patient talks a bit, chaplains recognize a familiar theme and are able to move forward more quickly.

LS: Yes, and they put labels on it. And that's not meant as a box but as a guide to make the pastoral care process more efficient. They are not creating pigeonholes into which they stuff patients, but the labels help the chaplain talk about it in somewhat of a definitional way. It gives chaplains tools that are parallel to other clinicians and they can talk something of the same language. It levels the playing field because chaplains are doing the same sorts of things as the other health care professionals except within their area of expertise.

Editor: So this sounds like there are various spiritual syndromes that chaplains can recognize and categorize. I guess physicians would call them syndromes.

LS: Right.

Editor: These categories would be similar to the kind of thing presented in the Diagnostic and Statistical Manual of Psychiatry. Chaplains have these broad categories in mind that are frequently found within a patient population and after a few clues from the patient, they can ask about characteristics of spiritual distress that are usually related.

LS: Right. The patient starts telling me a story and what they say contains clues and they direct me to ask some further questions because I have a sense of what's coming up next.

Editor: Exactly.

LS: And then chaplains become a more active partner in these conversations. To put this in a scientific perspective, the process starts out like qualitative research. A half dozen patients tell the story of their illness experience and chaplains identify the themes. After gathering the themes, chaplains go on to empirical research, testing whether a larger patient population validates them.

Editor: Yes.

LS: That's what the chaplains who developed *The Discipline* have done except not in a rigidly scientific manner. They've done it by sitting down and talking with each other. They have developed their own intentional processes.

Editor: So, now let's turn to how you are adapting the process for yourself. How are you developing it?

LS: Well, so far somewhat roughly. Right up front I am clearer with students about what I expect in a pastoral care visit–it is a mini research project. In a pastoral visit, the patient starts by telling a story, but the chaplain is using a research perspective to gather information. Students begin to identify familiar themes present in that information, themes that are problems for the patient. And, for students, those themes lead to theories about pastoral interventions. After awhile these theories need to be validated and if other chaplains agree that these theories are plausible and not just the wild ideas of one chaplain, then a plan is developed that constitutes an intervention. If the patient agrees that their concerns are dispiriting them and that they need more spiritual strength to meet their medical crisis, then the chaplain implements the plan. The patient then hopefully experiences benefits that constitute an outcome. Does the patient have more energy? Is the patient happier, more willing to cooperate with the medical regime? Students need to identify an outcome of some type. If no outcome is apparent, then they need to go back to the beginning. The assumption is that the theory was wrong in some way and the student starts listening again to develop a new theory and repeat the process.

Now sometimes the student only has the option of a single pastoral visit because the patient is not in the hospital very long. At other times, many visits are possible and necessary, as in the case of burn or oncology patients. I believe that every time I make a pastoral care visit on a new patient, I am conducting a miniature research project. The actual extent of the project depends on the patient's needs, how long they are in the hospital, and the help they request.

But looking for outcomes–that's another thing, the outcome aspect is something that I found very helpful when I talked with Chaplain Lucas. The medical community is looking for outcomes; that's their focus. And I know that, as a Director of Pastoral Care, when students talk about outcomes, that weds the entire department more strongly to the clinical environment. We're talking parallel language to the other clinical disciplines. An outcome can be related to the total hospital experience of a discharged patient or to a patient who had a better dying experience. We don't have to talk the same language but we're using parallel language to describe what we're about. This outcome focus, especially for CPE students, builds their confidence that they can contribute to the clinical team.

Editor: So they can focus on their contribution. It's not so nebulous.

LS: Yes, students are able to say at least to themselves, "I have a place; I'm not just here in case some support is needed. I'm not an outsider fighting for my place; I have a place and I can tell people what it is." That builds confidence and authority, two important CPE issues. It also gives students an opportunity to integrate their own theological descriptions of the patient's experience and their interventions.

Editor: So it gets the student past this pervasive stance, "I'm a friendly visitor wandering around to see how I might be helpful."

LS: That's right. And it is also important for a Pastoral Care Department Director like myself because I can now clarify for hospital administration why they need chaplains rather than parish clergy who simply come in and talk.

Editor: Or volunteers.

LS: Especially volunteers. When I worked in Canada we got rid of volunteers because it simply became too confusing. Volunteers, parish clergy, and chaplains all visited patients and administration began to wonder why chaplains should be employed. It became too difficult for administration to see clearly that chaplains were doing something more and different.

Editor: So you have pretty much taken what Chaplain Lucas and his team have developed right into your clinical context? You've not overhauled it in a big way?

LS: Well, yes and no. Because of some peculiarities in this institution and the department, I have integrated it mainly through the CPE program. There has been some resistance and mixed acceptance from staff. The morning I left to visit St. Louis, I was talking to one of the denominationally linked pastoral staff members about it and the response was that it would never fly here.

Editor: What kind of resistance do you get from students?

LS: None.

Editor: None?

LS: None. *The Discipline* diminishes confusion about what chaplains do and what their role is in the nursing unit. The first couple of weeks of the program are far less confusing for the students. There are still issues about how the individual student can become part of the team on the unit, but they appreciate the structure. They still have anxieties, "How do I enter a room when I'm not wanted, when a patient didn't ask for me?" There are still all sorts of other anxieties going on. However, they now walk into a room with a structure. This is particularly important this year because all of my residents never had prior CPE and so I had to start Introductory CPE with them.

Editor: I see.

LS: The structure provided by *The Discipline* encourages students to feel, "I know what I'm doing." It does not seem to lead to an over-confidence that interferes with learning; it seems to support learning.

Editor: "I know what I'm here for."

LS: Right. "What I'm here for and I have a process in hand to guide me." So there is noticeably more confidence in the early weeks even though a lot of learning still needs to happen. It has not changed the amount of supervisory work, but it affects the attitudes of students as they begin ministry on the nursing units.

Editor: Any particular ways in which *The Discipline* has influenced how you assign students to various units or your CPE curriculum? Is there any influence on what didactics you incorporate?

LS: I'm doing less of a psychological type of didactic than I've done before and doing more didactics along these clinical lines in terms of identifying patient themes. As a matter of fact, I've been working on a seminar that I have been using and refining all along but fits better within the context of *The Discipline*. This seminar focuses on, "How do you operationalize spirituality?" We discuss terms like hope, despair–about 18 terms altogether. Each week we create a polarity, like hope and despair. The students then look for this polarity in their patient conversations and bring back patient illustrations of what they found. In discussion, we ask, "What words do patients use when they are hopeful or what words do they use when they're despairing?" "What kind of experience do they describe, what kinds of thoughts do they have about themselves and their life experience?" We try to operationalize these words in terms of flesh and blood.

Editor: And you tend to do that weekly?

LS: That's weekly, right. In the residency it lasts for two units because of the number of terms that are used.

Editor: Can you give some examples of other terms that are used besides hope and despair?

LS: Let me pull out the book! Hope, despair, peace, turmoil, communion, alienation, perseverance, defeat, acceptance, shame. I don't remember just when, but I came across the Galatian passage where Paul talks about the fruits of the spirit: love, joy, peace, long suffering, etc., etc. All of the sudden it hit me! Paul is doing clinical assessment here. That's what I started with. And based on Oglesby and Hiltner, I started asking myself what a strong spirit looks like, what its characteristics are. I compared that to characteristics of a dispirited person, what is the opposite of hope. And that's how that developed. The students identify words based on their individual traditions and then we discuss them in the group setting. This builds consistency within the group and also makes sure that the students talk about these concepts in a manner that doctors and nurses understand. So we don't talk about things just in theological jargon, theological terms.

Editor: Let me turn the conversation to the future of *The Discipline.* What do you think is its future?

LS: My personal feeling is it has to be the future of pastoral care. In one of the presentations he made to his hospital, Chaplain Lucas talked about redefining how pastoral care is provided and how we need to be careful not to throw out the baby as we're changing the bath water. I believe we do have to be careful. One of my students was talking with an elderly physician who still works in hospital half time and she was lamenting to the student that care is so easily lost in medicine these days because it is so scientific. Physicians give a diagnosis, prescribe a medication, and move on. Physicians aren't spending time with their patients. And then she began to talk about the importance of pastoral care because chaplains bring the human touch to the bedside. That human touch is the baby that we don't want to throw out. *The Discipline* allows us to keep that, as I was talking about earlier, to structure what we do in a manner that is parallel to the other major disciplines, specifically medicine and nursing. *The Discipline* provides us a better chance to be equal partners in healing with them and we can keep the human touch.

Editor: You might be interested in the literature about whether health-care professionals really should care about their patients or whether it is sufficient or, in fact, mandatory that they only act like they care but they really don't. Some serious ethical discussions have taken place about whether it's unethical to actually care about patients. The arguments take an interesting form because it's quite clear that health care professionals can not equally care about all the patients equally and this creates discriminatory practice. In some ways that discussion seems symptomatic of current health care dilemmas.

LS: It's interesting. I'm not aware of that dialog. That would be interesting to read.

Editor: I have worked my way through my questions. Anything else you want to say about *The Discipline*? It sounds like you will continue to work at adapting it; the process seems to have taken root with you.

LS: Very much so. Like I said, it gave me a structure to work with concerns that troubled me. I know some of my colleagues are troubled by the same concerns and are excited about what Chaplain Lucas has done. I say "some" because it's a mixed bag and some feel it's too structured and it is throwing out the baby. I feel it gives us further inroads to be equal partners during a time of tremendous change in medicine. These changes mean that Herbert Benson can regularly draw huge crowds to his seminars around the country. Chiropractic is entering into dialog again with medicine along with many alternative medical practices. These are changing times. My feeling is that *The Discipline* puts us in a prime position, that it gives us a chance to strengthen our relationship to medicine.

I know of two institutions that merged spiritual care departments. The Pastoral Care Directors of the two original institutions responded quite differently. The one lamented that spiritual care was loosing strength and not getting sufficient attention. But this Director was not talking about how spiritual care could be integrated into the medical community. Obviously, it was his colleague who became Director of the merged departments. He talked about the need to create partnerships with other professionals, showing leadership in defining spiritual care for the future. I believe *The Discipline* helps us with that task.

Using *The Discipline*
for Integrative Ministry Formation

Fred L. Smoot, PhD, BCC

SUMMARY. One United Methodist Annual Conference has begun a program of ministry formation education for probationary, first-appointment ministers in conjunction with Emory Clergy Care, Atlanta. This program uses an adaptation of *The Discipline* as an integral part of their ongoing formation education. Participants have learned the basics of planned pastoral care delivery, family and congregational systems thinking and self-supervision. Using *The Discipline,* they have been effectively adapting it to their local church settings and ministries.

KEYWORDS. Clergy, spiritual formation, pastoral care

INTRODUCTION

The United Methodist Church operates on an appointive system. The Bishop places ministers in the churches within an Episcopal area, and they serve there until they are appointed elsewhere. Under the United Methodist system, these ministers are placed in a probationary status as "Commissioned Ministers," usually for a period of three to

---

Fred L. Smoot is Director, Emory Clergy Care, 3700 Crestwood Parkway, Suite #270, Atlanta, GA 30096 (E-mail: Fred_Smoot@emory.org).

five years. It is a time of adjustment and learning, and often experienced as alien to their seminary experience. Often, they must practice more self-discipline and self-initiative. They learn practical church administration, practice real life congregational care, lead worship and practice the priestly arts of baptizing, confirming, marrying and burying their parishioners. Often, these new ministers become lonely, fearful, disillusioned and tired. They need the support of peers for sustenance, the care of a mentor for confidence and refinement and some intense continuing practical ministry education to make applicable much of what they learned in seminary (Blackmon & Hart, 1990).

Some annual conferences have developed programs for addressing these identified needs. The Missouri East Annual Conference, through its Ordained Ministries Team, has worked out a series of intense retreats which have been structured to specifically address and embrace them while keeping to a minimum the minister's time away from the parish. Because these retreat gatherings are known in advance, churches and ministers can plan ahead for them in the church calendar, and possible disruption caused by the minister's absence are minimized for all concerned. The Ordained Ministries Team has developed this approach in conjunction with Emory Clergy Care, and The United Methodist General Board of Higher Education and Ministry.

One learning module focuses on pastoral competence and the need for structure and accountability in parish pastoral care. The use of *The Discipline* was adapted to the parish setting with good results. Commissioned ministers report that their process of giving pastoral care and visitation has more form as well as structure and is markedly more effective in terms of good outcomes.

THE LEARNING CONTEXT

The commissioned minister's parish has formed the heart of the learning context. The parishioners are teachers as well as the receivers of care. Added to this natural learning crucible is the forum for processing and reflecting on ministry provided by the safety of the formation retreat setting comprised of peers, facilitators and observing mentors. This structure provides a rhythm of engagement, supervised reflection and support. These sessions have been led by a Clinical Pastoral Education Supervisor, who works with the individual presenting the case and the peer group as it processes together.

The first two retreats of the Formation Ministry Program invest initial sessions introducing the theory and operation of a disciplined approach to pastoral care in the parish. Leaders and participants have brought current situations from their ministries for consultation as well as supervision. Participants have sought how they could benefit their people with better service and a more theologically focused presence.

The group provides both "refinement" and "support" to the process. Absolute confidentiality is maintained in covenant. For example, any used written documents are collected and destroyed following the sessions. Process notes may be kept only if all identifying information is deleted.

The Pastoral Care Modules are one part of the entire retreat process. They have been experienced alongside other modules that inform the practice of ministry. This process forms a fabric of work during the retreat that can be replicated in the parish. Just as the retreat does not focus on just one aspect of ministry, but engages the participants in several aspects over a brief time, the learning of a discipline for doing pastoral care is done alongside many other skills and practices. Pointing this out to participants aids in the transfer of learning to the parish. It also raises the possibility that other ministerial practices might benefit from a disciplined, outcome oriented approach.

THE COMMON THREADS
OF FIRST TIME APPOINTMENTS

First appointments have some common threads. Usually they involve the pastor in serving more than one small congregation. Sometimes they are staff appointments to larger churches. The common thread that stands out for many participants is the compromised connection between the various groups (or congregations) the new minister serves. This complexity is a challenge that must be met early on. How the minister understands the nature of these group relationships is crucial for effective ministry. This has involved an assessment process. The hoped-for outcome is an effective work distribution pattern that embraces the spiritual needs, hopes and resources of these groups (Patton, 1990).

The Discipline asks, "Who are these persons–this family, this church, this work group? Identify their needs, hopes and resources." The aim of the formation program is to engage these new ministers around this question as they embark into new congregations and new responsibilities.

At one very real level, the aim of the parish based discipline process is to teach effective assessment skills. Much new work has been done on spiritual assessments for individuals, particularly individuals in crisis (Fitchett, 1993). However, the assessments are not only of individual spiritual needs but also of the families as well as the congregation as a whole.

Another common thread is the often open-ended nature of ministry, which is quite different from the rather tightly structured seminary experience. New ministers often report times when they didn't know what to do with their time, or that they were overwhelmed or underwhelmed, and were struggling to establish a good work rhythm. They knew to prepare a sermon, and to answer phone calls, and to call on those they knew were sick. But, how to do this within a disciplined framework was not taught to them. They need a framework for a pattern of continuous pastoral work that has evolving and specific outcomes. Perhaps this is the most difficult of all the issues facing new ministers.

Tied to this is the issue of professional and collegial accountability. Whether one works on a staff or in a three-point charge, holding oneself accountable for one's activities is crucial to effective ministry. Wesley's dictum, "Go not just to those who need you, but to those who need you most," points to the desired outcome of accountability. Associated with this is the need for accountability to those in authority. This accountability should be measurable and constant enough to promote confidence that one's work is accomplishing larger goals and not simply activity for its own sake.

Finally, the question, "When am I done for now?" haunts most new ministers. Often they experience ministry as a never-ending stream of unrelated, urgent and important activities. The form and shape of pastoral care activity often frustrates them because they see only small interventions or conversations in parishioner's lives and fail to place these in a larger context of meaningful objectives and follow-through. This frustration easily leads to avoidance of difficult pastoral care tasks and worse, to burn out from the boundary-less demands of some parishioners that appear to plague caring ministers. The practice of *The Discipline* ameliorates much of this frustration and encourages appropriate objective and limit setting.

TEACHING THE DISCIPLINE FOR THE PARISH SETTING

The parish is the ultimate learning crucible. In it, the new minister learns how to minister, either effectively or not. Three deficits of the parish learning environment are: (1) the lack of space and time to reflect on what one is learning, (2) lack of experienced support, a mentor, to assist choosing which options for ministry are most effective, and (3) the minister's reported sense of isolation from professional peers who can provide counsel and support.

Essentially, the task of learning *The Discipline* is a way of learning self-supervision. Among other things, it is a template of focused tasks that enable pastoral work to move forward in an orderly way, and result in effective ministry to individuals, families and church groups.

At the Ministry Formation Retreats, the participants gather and focus on a case from the parish brought by a group member. The presenting minister follows a pattern of work that asks the following disciplinary questions:

1. Who is the person in this narrative who is the focus of your care? What do you know about them demographically?
2. Assess the contextual situation and the person in front of you at three levels: Assess their needs, their hopes and their resources. What is your evidence for this assessment from your observation and conversation with those involved?
3. Using this information, can you assess their spiritual condition, by developing a "spiritual profile" that speaks to the following issues of spirituality:

- How does the holy function in this person's (family's) life? How does the person understand "the beyond in the midst of his/her current situation," and how does this effect daily living and coping with life's challenges?
- How does the person use hope to cope? Do they have a sense of "finding a way through" this current situation and/or life in general? How does hope function in their living day by day?
- What has meaning for this person? What does this person value that has some sustaining power for them. What do they "worship" or spend time "attending to"?
- How does this person participate in the community of faith, the civil community, the community of family? How does this person's personal community enrich or deplete their sense of life?

Using this profile information, one can begin to sense and articulate desired outcomes. This process involves taking the relationship to a level of mutual acknowledging, addressing and embracing the growth issues in the spiritual profile. The most important part of this phase is to *develop outcomes* that address the assessed profile of spirituality. Such mutually evolved outcomes are crucial to effective transformational ministry.

In the parish, new ministers have learned to think long-term as well as short-term, developmentally as well as interventionally. One long-term desired outcome, for instance, might be to effectively engage a family's spirituality resources over the life of the child rearing phase so that children grow from a literal faith to a more interpersonal one (Ivy, 1985). This might involve working with the family to insure its regular interface with the church school. It also involves insuring that the church school understands the importance of faith growth development, as opposed to simply teaching children Bible verses by rote without attachment to other learning objectives. It might involve the family becoming involved with the needy as well as getting to know some of the church's "spiritually enriched" members.

Designing "contributing outcomes" for the parish often challenges the norm, "the way we have always done it." It asks the parish educators and worship leaders to reflect on their task in the light of the real, concrete persons in front of them, rather than the imagined "normal family or individual." This approach leads to both anxiety and excitement. Persons report that they have reached new levels of involvement that make ministry "a new adventure daily." It refocuses activity and prioritizes it meaningfully. One student spoke for the group when she said after trying this with a few families in her church, "I know when I am through for the day with these people. We all rest better because we all believe we are on the right track." Her peers in the Ministry Formation program were both supportive and excited to try this in their own parishes. One of the most important steps in this process is to make sure that the outcomes are concrete and measurable, not vague but observable if they are achieved.

Contributing outcomes can also be sharpened through the use of the classical shepherding functions. Ministers can ask, "How is this desired contributing outcome healing? How is it sustaining? How is it guiding toward deeper faith growth and life?" (Hiltner, 1958).

It is then a short step to planning actions and/or activities that will move the outcomes toward completion. This planning has not been difficult if the prior steps have been carefully taken. Our formation ministers are currently still engaging this step in their learning. The question that has occurred most frequently had been around relating actions in ministry to desired outcomes.

The issue for many has been, "How do I know if my day to day actions contribute to the spiritual welfare of my people?" The search for focused actions that move *The Discipline* process forward toward spiritual growth and enrichment has demanded much more thoughtful encounters with parishioners. The assessment of what to look for in these persons over both the short and long haul is most challenging, and most rewarding. The whole aim of becoming "intentional" about ministry planning and action is not as easy as a "more concerned presence," yet such increased presence forms the basis of the kinds of effective actions that change lives. One learning about this step is that the pastor cannot rely only on "presence," or only on doing effective "ritual," or only on "preaching," or on classroom Christian education, but must creatively engage all the resources of the whole Church, both in planning and action. Ideally, the pastor must think in terms not only of the individual or the family directly involved, but also the larger faith community and civil community. Training in systems thinking is very helpful (Steinke, 1993).

The reflection process follows action. "What has happened as a result of these plans and our actions?" *The Discipline* takes a different turn in the parish, not because we cannot observe outcomes, but because the results might possibly have more impact on the community of faith than if done in a clinical setting. Again the richness of the parish is often overlooked in the reflective stage, yet it is here that our honesty about what can be claimed as results can have its biggest rewards. Disciplined reflection as moral attending, takes into account both what we have hoped would happen, and what we can observe and measure happening. The aim of such reflection/attending is to do the next right thing; it is risky and involves the practice of faith (Smoot, Yancey & Wagner 1999).

Such reflection enables a clearer view of the needs, hopes and resources of those to whom we minister, and we can then begin our new assessment of the situation with informed enthusiasm and clarity. At worst, what has not worked can be eliminated; what has worked can be noted. At best, we can celebrate our growth in the life of faith as God's people, and know we have participated somehow more consciously in the mystery of God's redeeming and refining love.

THE ACCOUNTABILITY FACTOR

Valuing accountability acknowledges that one shares responsibility with others, and that such sharing is essential to the well being of all concerned. In the parish, the covenanted use of *The Discipline* underscores the importance of mutual accountability of the minister to the congregation and its ministry. Reciprocally, the congregation is accountable to the minister as its ministry is led. Finally, all must practice mutual accountability with the larger church, whose undergirding support can be most effective in a climate of known priorities and focused direction and action.

At the heart of it, *The Discipline* teaches self-supervision in community. It develops leadership (Jones, 1993). It keeps the efforts of those involved focused on the spiritual priorities of the church's mission, and it measures the outcomes of those efforts for practical use to keep the church and its leaders in a healthy rhythm of assessment, planning and intentional reflection.

CONCLUSION

The Ministry Formation Program has used *The Discipline* to form a pattern of work for first appointment ministers as they develop their pastoral care ministries. The pattern has proven its usefulness in that many probationers in the group have reported that they have a clearer understanding of the needs, hopes and resources of the persons and congregations they serve. Envisioning and planning the long-term outcomes of their ministries has been shown to be as important as planning the short-term outcomes. The process has a human, predictable rhythm of assessment, action and reflection that allows for both error and success, and celebrates both as a part of the learning life of the church.

REFERENCES

Blackmon, R. & Hart. A. (1990). Personal growth for clergy. In R.A. Hunt, J.E. Hinkle & H.N.Malony (Eds.), *Clergy assessment and career development* (pp. 36-42). Nashville: Parthenon Press.

Fitchett, G. (1993). *Assessing spiritual needs; a guide for caregivers*, Minneapolis: Augsburg Press.

Hiltner, S. (1958). *Preface to pastoral theology* (pp. 89-172). Nashville: Abingdon.

Ivy, S. S. (1985). The structural developmental theories of James Fowler and Robert Kegan as resources for pastoral assessment. (Doctoral dissertation, The Southern Baptist Theological Seminary, 1985). (University Microfilms (1990). No. 1416).

Jones, E. E. (1993). Why should I change? A new paradigm for leadership. *Quest for Quality in the Church,* (pp.50-58). Nashville: Discipleship Resources.

Patton, J. (1990). Self evaluation through relational experience, In R.A.Hunt, J.E. Hinkle & H.N.Malony (Eds.), *Clergy Assessment and Career Development,* (pp. 123-128). Nashville: Abingdon.

Smoot, F. L., Yancey, V. J. & Wagner, T. J. (1999). An interdisciplinary approach to integrative professional education. *The Journal of Pastoral Care, 53, 2,* 139-156.

Steinke, P.L. (1993). *How your church family works; Understanding congregations as emotional systems,* Chicago: The Alban Institute.

Index

Numbers followed by "f" indicate figures.